GOD
PLEASERS

Becoming Modern Day Enochs

CHIQUIS HOWARD

WESTBOW
PRESS®
A DIVISION OF THOMAS NELSON
& ZONDERVAN

WestBow Press books may be ordered through booksellers or by contacting:

WestBow Press
A Division of Thomas Nelson & Zondervan
1663 Liberty Drive
Bloomington, IN 47403
www.westbowpress.com
844-714-3454

ISBN: 979-8-3850-2719-4 (sc)
ISBN: 979-8-3850-2720-0 (e)

Library of Congress Control Number: 2024912037

Print information available on the last page.

WestBow Press rev. date: 08/21/2024

CONTENTS

By faith [that pleased God] Enoch was caught up and taken to heaven so that he would not have a glimpse of death; and he was not found because God had taken Him; for even before he was taken [to heaven], he received the testimony [still on record] that he had walked with God and pleased Him (Hebrews 11:5 AMP)

DEDICATION

I would like to dedicate this book to the billions of God seekers and God pleasers who are emerging as God's new army. May this book help bring a greater hunger and revelation of what it is to be madly in love with our Creator and Father!!!

PREFACE

Do you ever wonder what words will be carved on your gravestone? Or what few phrases will summarize your entire life? Even better, what will you be remembered for when you step from this short life into eternity? I must confess that I have been considering these questions for years. For a while, I thought hearing the words of my Father, "Well done my good and faithful servant," would be the highlight of everything. However, a few years into my spiritual journey, I began noticing a pattern where God was often encouraging his faithful children with the words, "I am pleased with you." There is no doubt these are wonderful words to hear, especially coming from the Father.

This set me off into discovering the meaning behind it. I found myself asking questions like, What does it really mean to please God? Why and how is it that some people are able to please Him? Do I please Him through the small things I do on a daily basis, like when I do or say the right things? Or, maybe, is it just my company that brings pleasure to Him?

This is where Enoch's story comes into play. Although very little is written about him in the Bible, his reputation of pleasing God is undeniable,

> *...For before he was taken away, he was approved as one who pleased God. (Hebrews 11:5 CSB)*

I had to know more. What was it about Enoch that captured God's heart? For many years now, through prayer and studying the

Bible, I have sought to discover the answers to this mystery. And in so doing, I have concluded that there is one phrase, more than any other, that I want written on my tombstone...

Here lies a God Pleaser!

INTRODUCTION

We live in a culture where self-seeking behavior is applauded, sought after, and viewed as a high priority. Some go so far as to think our purpose on earth is to take part in all that brings pleasure. Their life motto is *pleasure at all costs*. This is not surprising since this train of thought has been ingrained in most of us since we were young. We are literally being bombarded by it from every direction, including the entertainment industry, social media, and the education system. We often hear comments such as "live for pleasure" or "do what feels good." And if we are honest, many of our decisions are based on whether something gives us pleasure. If it doesn't, we have no problem replacing it with something that will.

Not surprisingly, this same way of thinking has been transferred into our relationship with God. We expect to snap our fingers at him and He becomes our personal genie. When the answers don't come fast enough or the way we want them, we walk away from God without a second thought. As a result, we end up missing out on everything that is true, real and good; all because we have believed the lies of living life for our own pleasure and self-seeking gratification. In other words, we have become a "me" society. We take advantage of people left and right in order to meet our needs or whims. How else can we explain most violence and crime taking place on our streets, other than a person wanting something at all costs?

Just a couple of weeks ago I read a foreign news article of a wealthy young man who proposed marriage to a lady whom he grew up knowing from his same social circle. When she refused his marriage proposal, in a state of rage, he kidnapped her, abused her and then proceeded to kill her. I wish this was not a true story, or at least an isolated one, but unfortunately, it is only one of many such injustices we hear about often. This is a result of a "me" society; a self-seeking, pleasure-driven culture! The Bible warns us that in the last days there will be an increase of wickedness:

> *But understand this, that in the last days there will come times of difficulty. For people will be lovers of self, lovers of money, proud, arrogant, abusive, disobedient to their parents, ungrateful, unholy, heartless, unappeasable, slanderous, without self-control, brutal, not loving good, treacherous, reckless, swollen with conceit, lovers of pleasure rather than lovers of God, having the appearance of godliness, but denying its power. Avoid such people. (2 Timothy 3:1-5 ESV)*

Is it possible that God is taken by surprise with such depravity and we are now doomed? On the contrary, our Father, the King, is always ahead of the game. And better yet, He has a plan! The book of Romans tells us that wherever sin increases, there is more than enough grace to triumph (Romans 5:20 TPT). In the midst of all this chaos, God has a God-proof plan; a strategy which might surprise you. But trust me, it's a great one!

> *The entire universe is standing on tiptoe, yearning to see the unveiling of God's glorious sons and daughters! For against its will the universe itself has had to endure the empty futility resulting from the consequences of human sin. But now, with eager expectation, all creation longs for freedom from its slavery to decay and to experience with us the wonderful freedom coming to God's children. (Romans 8:19-21 TPT)*

So what is this great master plan? It is none other than "you" and "me." Wild isn't it? You may have been thinking you were going to go hide in a cave while the Davids show up with their slingshots ready to kill the giants. Instead, God is including us in his timely and strategic plan. He is giving us the slingshot and calling us into the battlefield!

We are in a new season when God is inviting his children to enlist into his army created to bring heaven down to earth! This supernatural, invading army will trample everything that is not aligned with heaven and restore God's intended beauty. This same army, which has been asleep for way too long, is waking up, sharpening its weapons and shining its armor. This army is unlike any we have ever seen or heard of. It is the very one that all of creation has been yearning for. This new militia will be made up of those who have one aim...to please their Commander in Chief, Jesus! They are a people willing to lay down their pleasure-seeking lives for something greater, ushering in God's wonderful freedom and life. Will you join this army known as the God Pleasers? Will you become a modern day Enoch?

CHAPTER 1

And **Enoch walked with God**: and he was not; for God took him

GENESIS 5:24 KJV

I n recent years I have been fascinated by this man named Enoch; a man of whom very little is known or written about in the Bible. And yet, what little is written speaks volumes and begs to be unveiled. I must confess that for years I read right through those few verses without a double take. It was not until I became eager in learning how to please God that I began searching out Enoch's fascinating life. And of course, it has been like looking for a lost pearl in the ocean, with lots of fill-in-the-blanks. For instance, in the book of Genesis we read,

> *And Jared lived an hundred sixty and two years, and he begat Enoch...And Enoch lived sixty and five years, and begat Methuselah: and Enoch walked with God after he begat Methuselah three hundred years, and begat sons and daughters: and all the days of Enoch were three hundred sixty and five years. And Enoch walked with God: and he was not; for God took him. (Genesis 5:18, 21-24 KJV)*

With the exceptions of a few other similar verses, this pretty much sums up what we know about Enoch. And as you can see, there are no juicy details or family drama to dwell on. We don't even know what he looked like, where he worked, or what he did for fun. It is no wonder we don't hear much about him. Out of all the children's Bibles I have read to my kids, I have yet to see a story about him. His name might pop up here and there, but it is mostly when going through the genealogies. He is definitely not one of the major players like Joseph, Moses or David, who are known for ruling and delivering nations or for killing giants.

Based on the scripture above, this is what we are told about Enoch: he was a 7th generation descendant of Adam and Eve, he had children, he lived to be 365, the name of his father was Jared, and the name of his oldest son was Methuselah. And although these things might be important and are written for a reason, for me personally, at first glance they seem unimpressive. They are definitely not something I would put down on a resume.

However, verse 24 blows my mind. In short, Enoch walked with God and suddenly disappeared! There was no body to bury, no good-bye letter to cry over ...he was just gone! I know you are probably thinking it sounds like a script from a sci-fi movie, yet this one was real and very original.

Something else worth noting here is that Enoch is the great-grandfather of Noah. Yes, the famous man from Noah and the Ark Bible stories. Noah was the only person in his day who dared to believe and obey God. As a result, he and his family were the only human survivors of the flood. Now this is worth bragging about!

Nonetheless, in the short few verses above, it mentions twice that Enoch walked with God. And normally when God repeats something in the Bible, it means He is trying to get us to pay special attention.

HABITUAL FELLOWSHIP

Some suggest that when God walks with someone, it means they are intimate and have a close relationship with him. But not to confuse this as something unique only to Enoch; in the next chapter, we see the same said about Noah:

Noah was a righteous man [one who was just and had right standing with God], blameless in his [evil] generation; Noah walked (lived) [in habitual fellowship] with God."
(Genesis 6:9 AMP)

By having the word habitual in brackets, the Amplified translation implies that walking with God for both Enoch and Noah, was a constant, customary event. I believe it is safe to conclude that both men knew God and walked in constant fellowship with him.

Some of my fondest memories living in Mexico as a missionary were my daily walks with God. As you can imagine, being single, young, and broke, was not without its trials and hardships. I literally had to trust God for everything from food, gas, and rent money, to protection and favor in a mostly male dominated culture. I am convinced that I would not have survived one year, much less eight, had God not held my hand every step of the way. But it was during my day-to-day walks with Jesus that I learned to rely on and trust him. It was then where I talked and fellowshipped with God, my best friend. There were things I could not always talk with people about, but He was always there for me. He understood me and He listened. And I too learned to recognize his voice, and sometimes even his whispers. Whatever I had going on in my day, I looked forward to our meeting times together where I could share with him what was in my heart or what I was going through. These walks literally became my life-line for those adventurous, yet challenging years.

During my first few years in Guadalajara, I did not live near a park, so it became my custom to walk to the downtown area. Guadalajara back then was said to be a city with over 5 million people. So as to be expected, my route was usually crowded and the streets were most often filled with chaotic drivers who were not shy in using their horns for every possible reason. But somehow I learned to tune it all out and still be in fellowship with my Father. I must have gotten pretty good at it because on one of my walks, I was so engrossed in my conversation with him, I did not notice a group of people blocking the sidewalk I was on. It was not until I was abruptly stopped in my tracks that I looked up, and saw a man who shoved a big microphone in my face, and another standing next to him holding a tv camera. Without a greeting or a warning, I was asked what I took or did for headaches. Without stopping to think, I immediately responded, "I pray." It took them, and me for that matter, a few seconds for the words to register. The interviewer proceeded to repeat my answer, "you pray?" Once I answered "yes," his following question was, "And does it work?" Once again my "yes" left him quiet. Without further words, they both stepped back and let me walk right through.

In the latter years of living in Guadalajara, I had a park not too far from where I lived. I went there almost every afternoon and walked its long, oval sidewalk over and over for hours just talking away with my sweet Friend. Up to this day, I could not tell you anything about the people that went there, or about any special events that took place in this large park. But I can definitely recall the anticipation I had every afternoon when it came time to put on my tennis shoes for my most important date of the day. Sometimes I could hardly wait to step onto the park's sidewalk so I could start unloading my heart to my most wonderful and caring Father. What fond and precious times those were for me.

For you see, something happens when we walk, talk and share our hearts with someone. We somehow become connected in a deep and intimate way. We learn to understand each other's values, dreams, and longings. We get to share each other's joys and even our heartaches. Most importantly, we develop a unique bond with that someone.

CONSISTENCY

Today I tend to spend more time with my Father during car drives than in walks. Nonetheless, as the scriptures above suggest, it is the consistency of doing something with someone which creates that special bond. And when that someone is no other than God himself, what a wonderful opportunity we are given to get to know him. We can become people much like Enoch and Noah, men and women who walk with God.

To expand on this a little more, let's consider what Genesis says after Adam and Eve ate of the fruit of the garden,

And they heard the voice of the LORD God walking in the garden in the cool of the day... (Genesis 3:8 KJV)

From this scripture verse we can see it is not only men and women who walk with God, but that God also walks with us. The word for walking in the above verses comes from the Hebrew word halak, which can be translated: to walk (literally and figuratively), continually, be conversant, and behave (self). Based on these definitions, walking with God can be compared to becoming familiar with someone while doing something consistently. In other words, what better way is there of getting to know someone than by doing something with them on an everyday basis. There are so many ways in which this can take place in our lives. Take for example, going to work, day in and day out, 5 days a week, 7-8 hours of your day. Whether we like it or not, we get to know the people we spend all that time with. This is no different than when we spend time with God. It is the daily and consistent walking with him that connects us in crucial ways.

BEING INTENTIONAL

As a young mother who enjoyed feeling productive, I had a hard time spending a large portion of my day driving kids back and forth to school and their after-school activities. I would often see cars drive by with little screens on the backseats playing videos at all hours of the day. As tempting as it was to buy a screen for my car, I felt challenged instead to not let those fleeting moments be wasted. That is when I became intentional during our drives. Of course it was not always smooth sailing. During some of our rides we learned to pray together, at other times we listened to each other's days and helped unload the hard parts of them. Some days one of us was upset (mostly me), and I am sure those were less than pleasant rides. But at other times, we drove in comfortable silence or with excitement and laughter. To my surprise, once the girls no longer needed me to drive them, I missed those special one-on-one opportunities. However, looking back, I can see the time we spent in the car together was instrumental for building a relationship we now enjoy at a whole, new level.

Close bonds do not just happen. Our relationships grow in depth when we become intentional about the time we spent together. It doesn't happen any other way. The same thing is true with our relationship with God. We must be intentional and purposeful with every opportunity we have to be with him.

I have been around people who think relationships should be in a continual honeymoon stage. Of course, I cannot blame them for wishing such, especially when we live in a world that can easily overload us with stressors. However, those relationships can only go so far and for so long, before reality hits. Part of getting to know someone and becoming close to them comes from having lived through hard moments together. It takes the good, the bad and the ugly to really bond with someone. If we become selective, instead of constant when knowing someone, it will become a more superficial connection. Our relationship with God is no different. In our daily time with God we need to be willing to weather the ups and downs of our most crucial relationship.

WALKING WITH GOD

Walking with God also suggests living a life pleasing to him. According to verse 9, Noah was a just, righteous and blameless man. In the Book of Hebrews we also read how Enoch walked in a manner pleasing to God. Can you imagine living your life in a way that delights God? Of all the things we could leave our children and their descendants with, I cannot imagine anything greater than the legacy of walking with God. And both Enoch and Noah did just that!

I wonder if Enoch's heritage and lifestyle is what caused Noah to want to follow in his footsteps by walking with God. Could this be the reason Noah was able to endure the evil around him and still maintain a righteous, pleasing relationship with God? Is this what allowed him to hear God clearly and carry out his plan to build an ark? Have you ever considered what would have happened if Noah had not been the man he was when God was getting ready to destroy the earth? It's a sobering thought, isn't it? And to say it was the end of the earth was not an understatement. Lets look at Genesis:

> The LORD regretted that He had made mankind on the earth, and He was [deeply] grieved in His heart. So the LORD said, "I will destroy (annihilate) mankind whom I have created from the surface of the earth—not only man, but the animals and the crawling things and the birds of the air—because it [deeply] grieves Me [to see mankind's sin] and I regret that I have made them." But Noah found favor and grace in the eyes of the LORD. (Genesis 6:6-8 AMP)

In verses 11 and 12 we can see why it was called an evil generation:

> The [population of the] earth was corrupt [absolutely depraved—spiritually and morally putrid] in God's sight, and the land was filled with violence [desecration, infringement, outrage, assault, and lust for power]. God looked on the earth and saw how debased and degenerate it was, for all humanity had corrupted their way on the earth and lost their true direction.

When I read this, it absolutely amazes me to see Noah being a righteous man in the midst of such evil. One translation reads, "But Noah was a pleasure to the Lord" (Genesis 6:8 TLB). That does not just happen. Something must have transpired between Enoch and his great-grandson, Noah, to have him become someone God looked upon with pleasure in a world where evil dominated. The Bible does not tell us, but it makes me wonder if Enoch's son, Methuselah, and his grand-son, Lamech, continued the family tradition of walking with God. Methuselah, no doubt, had grown up seeing his father walking seemingly alone, yet often heard him talking and even laughing as if someone else was with him. When asking his dad about it, Enoch might have brushed it off as if it was common knowledge, yet ventured in responding something like, "I am just having my daily God-walk, son."

Just think what it would be like to grow up seeing this type of habitual relationship between your earthly father and heavenly One. This could easily become a lifestyle passed down from generation to generation. And if indeed Enoch's God-walks became a family tradition, I have to believe at the time no one suspected it would one day save the human race from being completely annihilated. And to think it all began with one man named Enoch, who chose to walk wholeheartedly with God.

<u>Prayer:</u>

Father, I want to become someone who walks with you on a daily and consistent basis. Will you please accompany me on this new journey?

CHAPTER 2

Those from every tribe of Israel who had
determined in their hearts
to seek the LORD their God followed the
Levites to Jerusalem to sacrifice to the
LORD, the God of their ancestors

2 CHRONICLES 11:16 CSB

While I was living in Guadalajara, there was a season where some friends and I went weekly to a nearby village to be with the children and shared Jesus with them. However, despite our trips being life-giving and rewarding, my favorite part of this memory comes from our rides back to the city. During our return trip, we consistently made it a habit to stop and eat at the food stands on the side of the highway. Their main specialty was homemade corn tamales, better known as tamales de elote. Somehow, these tamales were mixed and made to be sweet without any additional fillings and were kept steaming hot in their huge pots, always tasting freshly made. They were absolutely delicious!

Once I moved back to the States, I found myself longing for those same tamales. Not surprisingly, on my first visit back to Durango, Mexico, I was intent on having them again. My dear aunt and uncle, who we were visiting at the time, helped me to look high and low for them, but to no avail. Finally we discovered these special tamales were unique only to certain regions of Mexico.

A few years later when I was invited to a friend's wedding in

Jalisco, I was determined not to return to the States without having eaten at least one tamal de elote. When I mentioned my special craving to my friend, she graciously drove me to the area where I used to buy them, only to find out the place no longer existed. She made several calls to friends and family members, but no one knew where to get them. Having exhausted our ideas, we decided to recruit her fiancé, who then drove us all over the city of Guadalajara looking for these specific tamales. After driving for hours late into the night, as a very last resort, my friend's fiancé called his mom, who used to know a tamal de elote vendor. Sure enough, she reveled the location and the vendor was still there with her steaming pot half full with tamales. At last my exhausting quest for this delicacy was over, and my intense craving was fulfilled. I made sure to buy several tamales to last me for my entire stay...I savored every last bite.

WHERE THERE IS A WILL, THERE IS A WAY

I have to laugh when I think back on my story of tamales and what I put my dear aunt, uncle and sweet friends through. If I am honest about it, I find my behavior a bit embarrassing. Yet it goes to show me how once we determine something in our hearts, it is hard to deviate from it until we reach our goal. Simply follow a small child and observe what he will do in order to put his little hands on that cookie he has been eyeing hungrily. A child will go to unbelievable lengths to get his cravings satisfied.

This drive is not something we have to be taught. It resides within us all. I like to think of it as a special gene we are born with called determination. For example, a newborn baby, without any training, will instinctively cry and cry until he is fed or cared for. Even toddlers can cry nonstop until they get what they want. Then as soon as they get it, they can immediately stop crying, and even go straight into laughing. It's mind boggling. Who told them that if they persist they will get what they want? The truth is no one has to teach us that. I believe it is an essential, innate behavior God created us with. Without it, some babies might not survive due to their caretakers forgetting to feed them, or being clueless when they are sick and need help.

> *...So we must let go of every wound that has pierced us and the sin we so easily fall into. Then we will be able to run life's marathon race with **passion** and **determination**, for the path has been already marked out before us. (Hebrews 12:1 TPT)*

Let's transfer this tenacity gene into our relationship with God. Just as we have it in us to be persistent when it comes to our earthly desires or needs, we have it in us to be tenacious and unstoppable towards our pursuit for God. We need the same resolve in approaching our King as little Johnny does when he wants a certain toy and can think of nothing else. I have watched children throw tantrums, scream and fight tirelessly to get what they want. It is amazing to see the great lengths we will go through to obtain what we really want. This is the same type of pursuit we see in a love-struck man on his quest for his girl. Some claim to be willing to die, take a bullet, or cross the ocean just to be with them. And yet, as beautiful or touching as these passions are, they do not compare to seeking the true lover of our souls, Jesus.

CREATED IN HIS IMAGE AND LIKENESS

From Romans chapter 8, we can see that people falling in love and being willing to give their lives for others is a reflection of God's unconditional love for us.

> *There is no power above us or beneath us—no power that could ever be found in the universe that can distance us from God's passionate love, which is lavished upon us through our Lord Jesus, the Anointed One! (Romans 8:39 TPT)*

Jesus, our ultimate example in everything, has pursued us from the beginning of creation and continues doing so today. Whether we love him back or not, He is constantly chasing after us. I believe if we stop to listen to his voice, we will hear his constant 'I Love You's' directed at us.

> *For God so [greatly] loved and dearly prized the world, that He [even] gave his [One and] only begotten Son, so that whoever believes and trusts in Him [as Savior] shall not perish, but have eternal life. (John 3:16 AMP)*

Through it all, Jesus lived and moved on the earth as one fully determined to do the will of his Father. He was determined to speak the Truth to everyone He came across, including those who would want to silence him. Jesus was determined to heal the sick, give sight to the blind and cleanse the leper. He was determined to bind up the broken hearted, give hope to the hopeless and set the captives free. He was determined to reach the unreachable and touch the unlovable. Jesus was determined to love the children and teach us how to be like them. He was determined to train his followers to live in their God- given authority here on the earth. Jesus was determined to walk in humility as the son of man without denying his heavenly position as part of the Trinity. He was determined to please his Father above all else. And He was determined to love us by giving his life for us, dying on the cross, going to hell and then being raised from the dead so we could have eternal life with him.

Jesus knew the reason He came to earth was to take our place by paying the ultimate price for our sins and becoming a human sacrifice. He was fully aware when the time of his death was near that He could ask for help and in a moment's time be rescued from the horrible death that awaited him...

> *"Don't you realize that I could ask my heavenly Father for angels to come at any time to deliver me? And instantly he would answer me by sending twelve armies of the angelic host to come and protect us. But that would thwart the prophetic plan of God..." (Matthew 26:53-54 TPT)*

So I wonder, having known all of this beforehand, what is it that kept Jesus from giving up? What helped him endure to the end?

> *Looking unto Jesus the author and finisher of our faith; who for the joy that was set before him endured the cross, despising the shame, and is set down at the right hand of the throne of God. (Hebrews 12:2 KJV)*

The Passion Translation says it so beautifully,

> *...Because his heart was focused on the joy of knowing that you would be his, he endured the agony of the cross and conquered its humiliation...*

Jesus was determined to endure until the end because of the joy of knowing we would be with him. His life was no doubt always lived under a strong determination to obey the Father. He focused on the end result and not on the present sufferings. He is the one we must look to as the author and finisher of our faith. It is up to us now whether or not we choose to pursue him with everything in us until we too one day finish our course here on this earth.

AT WHAT COST?

There was a time in history, much like our present one, where one of Israel's kings, Jeroboam, instituted idol worship in ten of the northern tribes of Israel. He did not let God's priests and Levites worship or make sacrifices to the LORD God. As a matter of fact, he fired them and replaced them with people willing to compromise and do his bidding. Does this sound familiar? God followers who are not allowed to worship or congregate together? Bakers unable to create and sell beautiful wedding cakes due to their God-given convictions? Evil and violence being applauded, while the righteous are persecuted and even wrongfully sentenced? The level of depravity and corruption we are experiencing is unprecedented. If foretold, we might not have believed it.

Yet here we are living in a time very similar to Jeroboam's. Freedoms that we have taken for granted are being stripped right out of our hands. Good people are being replaced by those who would have us bow to their idols and submit to their evil and corruption. Here is a short account of the Israelites under Jeroboam's ruling:

> *For the Levites left their pasturelands and their possessions and went to Judah and Jerusalem, because Jeroboam and his sons refused to let them serve as priests of the LORD. Jeroboam appointed his own priests for the high places, the goat-demons, and the golden calves he had made. Those from every tribe of Israel who had **determined in their hearts** to seek the LORD their God followed the Levites to Jerusalem to sacrifice to the LORD, the God of their ancestors. (2 Chronicles 11:14-16 CSB)*

In this verse, to be determined implies having made a firm decision and resolving not to change from it. The Israelites, who had once served God, were now faced with new imposed restrictions placed on them by their new leadership. They were practically forced to make a decision as to whether they would worship God or worship idols. There was no middle ground. And to make no decision was to make a decision.

There are times in our lives when change becomes inevitable and compromising is not an option. Such was the time for the Israelites under Jeroboam's rulership and for us under our present leadership. For the first time ever in our country, we can have serious consequences if we make a stand for God. We must be silent and accept an ungodly agenda being shoved down our throats or potentially face the backlash by those in power. More than ever before in our country's history, we must count the cost of following God and not worshiping the "idols" of the cultural elites.

Verse 14 tells us that those who had determined in their hearts to seek the Lord left practically everything behind, including their lands and possessions, and moved away. I cannot imagine this was an easy decision for the Israelites. Throughout the Old Testament we can see that land was not treated as a commodity, but as a priceless inheritance, meant to be protected and kept within the family line. It was not like our present culture where we have no problem uprooting to a different city or state for reasons like jobs, schools, friends, etc. To the Israelites, who were determined to follow after God, this meant they were willing to lose everything they held dear in order to keep their innate freedom to worship their Creator.

This hard decision began with a few, the priests and Levites, who were the religious leaders of their time. But soon those who also purposed in their hearts not to contaminate themselves with the sins of idolatry followed them. They too left everything behind and moved to Jerusalem where they could worship and serve God freely.

Much like the Israelites, we are being forced to choose whether we will follow God in the face of persecution and potential loss. May we find courage from those willing to leave earthly comfort and safety behind and determine to follow our amazing God at all cost.

DESPERATE FOR HIM

There is a story in the New Testament about a woman whose daughter was being tormented by evil spirits. This is an account of her desperate plea to Jesus for help:

> *He encountered there a Canaanite woman who screamed out to Him, "Lord, Son of David, show mercy to me! My daughter is horribly afflicted by a demon that torments her." But Jesus never answered her. His disciples said to Him, "Why do you ignore this woman who is crying out to us?" Jesus said, "I've only been sent to the lost sheep of Israel." But she came and bowed down before Him and said, "Lord, help me!" Jesus responded, "It's not right for a man to take bread from his children and throw it out to the dogs." "You're right, Lord," she replied. "But even puppies get to eat the crumbs that fall from*

the prince's table." Then Jesus answered her, "Dear woman, your faith is strong! What you desire will be done for you." And at that very moment, her daughter was instantly set free from demonic torment. (Matthew 15:22-28 TPT)

At the time this verse was written, a Canaanite person was considered a Gentile. It was also common knowledge that Jews and Gentiles did not associate with each other. Mark 7:26 says that she begged Jesus repeatedly, for which the disciples were asking him to send her away. However, Jesus was not moved by any of it; the woman, the chaos, nor the disciple's appeal. He was more interested in finding a way to reach her.

This desperate, needy woman was not only ignored, but even when she said the right things, like calling him Lord, Jesus remained silent and unmoved. He then proceeded to tell her it is not right to give her what belonged to the Jewish people, and to top it all off, He insults her by calling her a dog.

Was Jesus really that mean-spirited and indifferent? Or could it be that in doing so, He was trying to uncover her level of faith? She seemed desperate to have her daughter set free, but would she receive from a foreigner or would she walk away as soon as she was ignored and insulted? Would she humble herself enough and take whatever He gave her, even if it meant only crumbs off of a table?

It could have been so easy for her to become offended and write Jesus off. How many times have we allowed offense towards others or God because things did not go the way we hoped? We can be so quick to judge based on circumstances that we end up forgetting the truth of God's faithfulness and goodness. Sometimes it is not until we become desperate that we are willing to put aside all pride and surrender at his feet.

How refreshing it must have been to find that none of Jesus' rebuffing moved her or deterred her from pursuing him for her daughter's healing. She refused to be offended by Jesus and instead, came to a place of total surrender. She knew only that Jesus had what she needed. She was hungry, not necessarily for the crumbs, but she was willing to take them if it was all He would give her. She was not going for plan B or C. Jesus was her only plan!

> *Blessed are the humble, for they will inherit the earth.*
> *Blessed are those who hunger and thirst for righteousness, for*
> *they will be filled. (Matthew 5:5-6 CSB)*

I know life can be rough, and for many these past few years have been unlike anything we have seen. But if it is not COVID-19 and all that is attached to it, there will always be something coming at us, simply because we have an enemy who is out to "steal, kill and destroy" (John 10:10). However, it is what we do when these attacks come that makes all the difference.

When we are under attack, will we hide in despair hoping someone else steps in and helps? Or will we be like the Canaanite woman and say, "I don't care about our cultural differences, your name calling, or the fact you are trying to get rid of me. I am not leaving until I receive what I came for."

I think God is truly pleased when we are so confident of his character that we refuse to be put off or offended by how He responds to us. When we persevere through our own doubts and discomforts and continue to seek God for an answer, He can't help but respond.

STOPPING SHORT

So many times, we stop just short of victory. We begin a little hungry for more of God but end up settling for a small bite instead of the full meal. We grab a mere sermon, a good book, or a moment of worship, without ever allowing our spirits to reach a place of true hunger. My kids were good at this. They took any opportunity to fill themselves with snacks that left them too full to eat their main meal. Instead of waiting long enough in God's presence for the full course, we often stop at the appetizer and count it good enough. Just as our bodies can only handle snacks for so long before nutritional deficiencies set in, our spirits can no longer afford to live like this. We must desire ALL that He has for us and not settle for anything less!

"Yes, Lord," she said, "yet even the dogs eat the crumbs that fall from their masters' table." (Matthew 15:27 CSB)

What if the Canaanite woman allowed Jesus' seemingly casual indifference stop her from moving forward and getting the healing her daughter so desperately needed? What if his name calling and apparent insults were beyond her, and as a result, she turned back just seconds before Jesus was about to heal her daughter?

I think often we give up too easily or too fast. We say we want more of God and desire to please him, but then we give up right before He is ready to start talking with us and revealing his heart.

We have what it takes to win and overcome every time. We were made to be strong and tenacious under any circumstance. We were created to be just like our Father, sons and daughters with unflinching determination. All we have to do is purpose with all our hearts to seek and pursue God no matter what the cost is. He is so worth it!

Prayer:

My heart is yours Lord, I surrender it all to you! I am determined to seek and pursue you with every fiber of my being. I am determined to walk in the path which is most pleasing to you.

CHAPTER 3

By faith [that pleased God]

Enoch was caught up and taken to heaven so
that he would not have a glimpse of death; and
he was not found because God had taken him;
for even before he was taken [to heaven], he
received the testimony [still on record] that
he had walked with God and pleased Him

HEBREWS 11:5 AMP

U p to this time, no one in the Bible is mentioned being caught
up and taken into heaven without first experiencing death.
Upon reading this verse, we can conclude that it did not just
happen. Enoch was not taken up by pure happenstance. This was
intentional. What was the important ingredient? Faith. The fact the
book of Hebrews mentions faith in connection with Enoch makes
me question what this faith that pleases God is all about. How could
Enoch, who lived way before we had the faith chapter of Hebrews
11, have walked in faith and pleased God with it?

When writing this book, I was hoping to skip the whole topic of
faith simply because of how it has been twisted and abused in some
circles. I have met good meaning people who have been deeply hurt
by the so-called faith movement. Nevertheless, since one of the few
times Enoch is mentioned in the Bible happens to be in Hebrews 11,
I realized that pleasing God and walking in faith are interconnected.
Hebrews 11:6 says that without faith it is impossible to please God.

So rather than desiring to stay clear of it, I was compelled to dive deeper yet.

The topic of faith can be intimidating due to its broadness. It is no secret that we all have faith in something or someone, seen or unseen. For example, when I go to sit on my little comfy chair, I have faith that it will hold me. On another note, some people equate being religious as being a person of faith. So what is faith? A quick google search says that faith is trust, confidence, optimism, hope, etc. It all sounds good, however, after reading Hebrews 11:6, I am sure that God has plenty more to say about it. So why not go straight to its source? My favorite definition is at the very beginning of this chapter. Its short version comes from the King James Translation:

> *Now faith is the substance of things hoped for, the evidence of things not seen. (Hebrews 11:1 KJV)*

But to get a broader definition, let's read it from the Amplified Translation:

> *Now faith is the assurance (title deed, confirmation) of things hoped for (divinely guaranteed), and the evidence of things not seen [the conviction of their reality—faith comprehends as fact what cannot be experienced by the physical senses]. (Hebrews 11:1 AMP)*

TITLE DEED

I like that the Amplified Bible includes "title deed" as a definition. I can identify with a piece of paper that says clearly what belongs to me. The words, substance and assurance, are wonderful words, but in my mind they are somewhat abstract. Yet I have no trouble picturing a title deed and applying it to my present reality. In that same train of thought, the Bible is my title deed for all of God's promises.

To better illustrate this, here is an example from my earlier days attending a faith-based Bible center. Back in the 80's, my older brother and I attended the same Bible school while sharing a vehicle and an apartment. For several months I had a hard time finding a job, so we often found ourselves without enough money for food or rent. But we were learning to put God's Word into practice. So we decided to take advantage of our needs and put his Word to the test. We took scriptures such as:

"Again, truly I tell you, if two of you on earth agree about any matter that you pray for, it will be done for you by my Father in heaven." (Matthew 18:19 CSB)

And my God will supply all your needs according to his riches in glory in Christ Jesus. (Philippians 4:19 CSB)

Wherever it said "you" or "your" we inserted our names, making them our personal promises from the Father. More than once we took a piece of paper and wrote a contract with God. In the contract we stated our specific needs (ie: amount of rent money and the date it was due). We also wrote God's promises concerning our needs, such as the scriptures just mentioned, and at the bottom we both signed and dated it. We then taped the piece of paper, our "title deed," to a central location and made it a constant point to remind God and ourselves of what already belonged to us.

Sometimes when we were tempted to worry about how we were going to pay the rent, especially when the due date drew near, we instead made ourselves declare and thank God for the answers to our prayer and for his promises being fulfilled. It has been many years since we wrote those contracts, but to this day, I can testify that we never once went without our needs being met. Never once were we late in paying our rent. And never once did we starve.

Oh, how I love Faith! I cannot imagine where I would have been all those years if I had not ventured into a walk of faith. I definitely would not have finished school or gone into the mission field. But most importantly, I would have missed out on experiencing God's personal, loving care and faithfulness towards me. I can tell you story after story of God's goodness to us during those few hard years. There were times when we had nothing but saltine crackers, honey and butter in our kitchen, yet out of the blue, someone would invite us over to eat, having no clue how much we were in need of a decent meal. Once a group of young adults invited us to join them to go watch a movie. Before I had a chance to say 'no,' since we did not have money, my brother stepped in and said we would be there. Of course he had an ulterior motive in going. The girl he really liked was going to be there. I was frankly very nervous and I did not have faith for it. In my mind, this was a simple want, not a need. Nonetheless, we went.

When we arrived, we greeted those around us and followed them into the long line to buy the tickets for the movie with no money in our pockets. With each step we took, I became more concerned. What were we going to do when the cashier asked us to pay? How would we explain that we wanted a ticket but had no money to buy it? I could picture how embarrassing it was going to look. Ugh, that was so uncomfortable, yet I knew I was riding on my brother's decision and his obvious faith. We were almost next in line to the ticket window when the person in front of us turned around to tell us that someone had already paid for our tickets. Oh my, that was a close one! But what an amazing memory it left implanted in my brain. I got to experience firsthand a side of my Father I did not know. One which let me know He cares for every area of my life, not just for meeting my basic needs. He let me know He takes pleasure in his children trusting him, even for something that is solely for enjoyment.

DIVINELY GUARANTEED

"Now faith is the substance of things hoped for" (Hebrews 11:1 KJV). When mentioning hope, the Amplified Translation adds the definition in the context of being divinely guaranteed. Verse 5 tells us Enoch was translated into heaven by faith that pleased God. With that said, we can conclude that if there is faith which pleases God, there must also be faith which does not please him. But how can we know the difference? I believe the answer lies in the words, "divinely guaranteed." To be divine means to come from the power of God, a god or a divine entity. Therefore, by putting our hope in God's truth, we hold the title deed of whatever we are believing for.

For example, let's say you just received a bad report from the doctor. Whether or not you realize it, you are now faced with a decision to make. Will you believe the doctor's report or will you choose to trust God and put your hope in his Word concerning your healing? (1 Peter 2:24, Psalms 118:17). Our physical symptoms, such as pain, combined with a doctor's report, weigh pretty heavy in our culture. So much so, that if we are not rooted and grounded in God's promises, it is easy to believe those reports above God's.

When receiving a negative report, it is critical that our hope and trust be in the only one who is truly Divine, Jesus Christ, and not in our own strength, in others, or even circumstances. Only in Jesus and him alone can the impossible become possible. Through faith in him, our every need can be met, even healing. The question then goes back to whether or not we have taken the time to hear what God is saying about our situation. Are we even including him in the decision? Or has the doctor's diagnosis become the first and final say?

I remember a time when my mom was deathly ill, going in and out of the hospital, with a death sentence every time she was diagnosed. It was hard for me not to give in to fear and to the sadness of losing her after each report. But I also remember once the doctors would leave the room, without fail, mom would muster enough strength to renounce all the words that had just been spoken over her body contrary to God's promises. Her declarations would go something like this, "I do not receive those words. I break them off of me in the name of Jesus, and I confess Psalm 118:17 over me, that I will live and not die and I will declare the works of the Lord."

Mom was barely in her forties when the most any doctor gave her to live was 6 months...but God! Today, at 83 years of age, she is strong and healthier than most people I know. Her hair is still naturally black with very little gray, her vision and hearing are as good or better than mine. She is constantly taking care of people, cooking meals for the sick and even holding prayer meetings in her home.

It pleases God to see His children walk in faith, even if that faith is only the size of a mustard seed. God is not looking for us to have tree-size faith in order to work on our behalf. But we do have to start where we are. All the months Mom spent alone and sick in bed, she was building up her faith by reading the Bible and listening to Bible teaching tapes. That is why when she was faced with a bad report from the doctors, her hope was already on the "divine guarantees" of God's Word. Her mind was set on God's reality and not on man's.

Enoch too had to have faith in order to have a reputation of pleasing God. For without faith it is impossible to please him (Hebrews 11:16). Maybe it was his consistent walks with God, or maybe his constant interaction with him, but either way, we have to assume that he knew God well enough to know what pleased him. By walking in sync with God, Enoch's faith unleashed the miraculous in his life. His hope was on the divine, the things of God, and not on earthly limitations. He learned to please God through his faith. When this perspective is held, the natural realm has to give way to the manifestation of what we are believing for, whether it is finances, healing, protection, etc. We do our part in trusting and believing God at his Word, and He does his part...which is the impossible.

CONVICTION OF OUR REALITY

The second part of Hebrew's definition of faith is:

The evidence of things not seen [the conviction of their reality–faith comprehends as fact what cannot be experienced by the physical senses]. (Hebrews 11:1 AMP)

This is where it gets fun! First we choose to agree with what already belongs to us, our title deed, as promised in God's word.

Then we align our thoughts and trust in God's promises, his divine guarantees. But now, our conviction becomes our reality. In other words, we begin to experience as fact what we are believing for. In our hearts and minds our prayers are a done deal. The answer is no longer out there, somewhere in space. We arrive to a place where we are absolutely convinced that we have what we asked for. It is like a father telling his little child he is going to get him a bike. More than likely the son will take him at his word and not loose any sleep over it. He won't even wonder if his father can afford it. Instead, he is going to be telling his friends that his dad is getting him a bike, and will proceed to plan what he is going to do with it once he gets it. It is no wonder the Bible tells us to be like children (Matthew 18:3).

In my Mom's case, if you could see pictures of when she was bedfast, you would think it was a corpse. Dad had to wake her up many times just to make sure she was still breathing. But not so for Mom. She did not see herself dead. She had filled herself with God's Word so much so that it became her only truth. She did not consider the severity of her dying body and refused to agree with any death sentence spoken to her. Instead, she was fully convinced God was her healer and she was going to be raised from the death bed. So much so that she purposed to ride a bicycle as soon as she was healed. And that's exactly what she did!

> *Faith empowers us to see that the universe was created and beautifully coordinated by the power of God's words! He spoke and the invisible realm gave birth to all that is seen. (Hebrews 11:3 TPT)*

Once we are fully convinced that our prayer has been answered, a great indicator of our faith is how we speak and act. Have you ever had someone ask for prayer only to hear them talk afterwards as if nothing changed once the prayer was done? I think this type of unbelief is no different than the child asking his father to buy him a bike right after the dad had finished telling him he was getting him one. One of two things could be happening, we are not truly listening or we do not trust the person we are asking.

When choosing to believe and agree in God's promises, we must align our words and thoughts with them. Confessing his Word over our circumstances and declaring it as truth opens up the door of faith for the impossible to become possible. When we have been given a promise by someone who is all-powerful, trustworthy and faithful to his Word, and we choose to place our full confidence in him to bring it to pass, guess what? It will happen! God is not a man that He would lie. If He has said it, He will do it (Numbers 23:19). He just needs faith in the earth! He is literally and actively looking for someone with conviction and trust in him.

For the eyes of the LORD run to and fro throughout the whole earth, to show Himself strong on behalf of those whose heart is loyal to Him. (2 Chronicles 16:9 NKJV)

Prayer:

Here I am Lord, look no further! I choose to believe you at your Word. Please help my unbelief that I may be fully pleasing to You!

CHAPTER 4

Faith translated Enoch from this life and he was taken up into heaven! He never had to experience death; he just disappeared from this world because God promoted him. For before he was translated to the heavenly realm **his life had become a pleasure to God**

HEBREWS 11:5 TPT

P art of my intrigue over the life of Enoch has to do with wondering how he was able to live a life that pleased God. How does a man who lived many hundreds of years before the Bible was written know how to please God? Yet we know he does because God seals his approval by taking him to heaven without him experiencing physical death. From the verse above we know Enoch walked by faith, for without it, it would have been impossible for him to please God. This is confirmed on the following verse:

> But without faith it is impossible to [walk with God and] please Him, for whoever comes [near] to God must [necessarily] believe that God exists and that He rewards those who [earnestly and diligently] seek Him. (Hebrews 11:6 AMP)

PASSIONATELY SEEKING

As I was pondering on this verse, the latter part was highlighted, '...He is a rewarder of those who diligently seek him' (KJV). As God's children we are often told that we must seek God, which makes plenty of sense, because in order to know someone, we must seek them out and spend time with them. However, it is how we go about seeking someone that determines the type of relationship we will end up with.

If we really want to know someone, we are likely to put everything aside and prioritize that person. We might change our schedules to put them first. We may even change our talk, dress and behavior to try to impress them. I have to believe we have all experienced or been around someone who is 'love-sick.' I personally remember a certain girl in high school who was part of our friend-group. She was beautiful, sweet and fun to hang out with. Sadly though, our friendship did not last long, for as soon as she began dating a certain boy, she became practically non-existent to the rest of the world. This girl went all in. When I happened to run into her in the hallways, it was as if she did not even see me. She only had eyes for him. And if we were ever able to talk with her when she was alone, the whole conversation would be about him. That is a bit of an obsessive case, I know, but it happens.

Just as my friend had her full attention on her boyfriend and seemed to think of nothing else, shouldn't we too be passionately pursuing the lover of our souls? Isn't He worthy?

When we look at the word "seek" in the Bible, we find that most of the time it refers to prioritizing, being deliberate in following after, or giving attention to someone or something. However, the Greek word used in this verse, ekzeteo, goes deeper than that. In an effort to relay its intended meaning, most translations use the word diligently to accompany it. I personally like the Passion Translation's use of the word, passionately. As in, "...He rewards the faith of those who passionately seek him." This Greek word, ekzeteo, implies a seeking out, investigating, scrutinizing; or to crave. (Expository Dictionary of the Bible Words by Lawrence O. Richards)

So to say we are seeking God, it must be something greater than a casual meeting here and there. It needs to be something that we begin to require of ourselves. A driving passion for God that supersedes all others.

PARABLE OF THE PEARL

Heaven's kingdom realm is also like a jewel merchant in search of rare pearls. When he discovered one very precious and exquisite pearl, he immediately gave up all he had in exchange for it. (Matthew 13:45-46 TPT)

I realize this parable can go two ways when deciding who represents the merchant and the pearl. The point I would like to make includes both. Jesus, much like the merchant, gave up everything to purchase our freedom. Like any good merchant, He did his full research ahead of time. He knew exactly what to look for and what it would cost once He found it. Knowing all of it, He still chose to leave his place of glory in heaven as God, to become a human like us. And if that was not enough, He went through the horrendous torture and death on the cross, knowing that at any time He could have stopped it. He gave up all He had in exchange for us. Does it not make you wonder how, being fully human, He was able to endure all of it until the end? This next verse gives us a glimpse of how Jesus was able to follow through to the finish line:

Looking unto Jesus the author and finisher of our faith; who for the joy that was set before him endured the cross, despising the shame, and is set down at the right hand of the throne of God. (Hebrews 12:2 KJV)

Jesus is our ultimate example of what it means to count the cost, to leave everything behind, and to endure it all, in order to obtain the prize. What was his prize? We are his prize! We are the precious and costly pearl! Yet the price for him was everything He had!

On the other hand, Jesus can also represent the very precious and exquisite pearl for whom we are willing to give up everything. In this case, we are like the merchant in search of the one true King, Jesus. Having investigated and scrutinized all other options, we realize He is all we ever wanted. Actually, He is exceedingly more than we ever could have imagined or hoped for. One look at him and we are undone. Our search is finished.

As we become serious about pleasing God, we must count the cost, be willing to leave everything behind, and endure all. Our focus, our desire and our passion must turn to the only One who is worthy, Jesus.

RUNNING THE RACE

You've all been to the stadium and seen the athletes race. Everyone runs; one wins. Run to win. All good athletes train hard. They do it for a gold medal that tarnishes and fades. You're after one that's gold eternally. I don't know about you, but I'm running hard for the finish line. I'm giving it everything I've got. No sloppy living for me! I'm staying alert and in top condition. I'm not going to get caught napping, telling everyone else all about it and then missing out myself. (1 Corinthians 9:24-27 MESS)

I remember my junior year in high school when I decided to do track. I really did not like to run, but I needed the exercise and was bored, so I asked if I could join without doing the meets. My coach was pretty agreeable, other than he required I did one race the whole season. It has been a day or two since this took place, but I do remember taking this seriously. I didn't miss practices and I trained as hard as anyone on the team. It soon became easy to do two laps around the football field for warm-up, a whole hour or two of training, and two additional laps for the warm-downs. I counted the cost and realized I could definitely do the 800 meter run at a home meet.

Well, the day of the meet came and I thought I was ready. I mean, the race's total was equivalent to my everyday warm-up. But to this day, I do not know what happened, other than if it had not been for a dear friend cheering me on at every corner, I probably would not have finished the race. It was the most unbearable 800 meters of my life. I could hardly finish the first lap, much less the second one. I had to will my whole body and mind across the finish line. I had to beat my body and set my face like flint (1 Corinthians 9:27, Isaiah 50:7). Needless to say, I was not the first to arrive, but neither was I the last. Most importantly, through much straining and striving, I finished the race.

I know this is no comparison to Paul's race, or the price Jesus paid, still, it reminds me that in everything worth doing there is a cost. And sometimes it is harder than we anticipate. Sometimes it catches us unaware. We might face every obstacle possible trying to get us out of the race, yet our focus must stay true to the finish line.

We may not know the details of Enoch's life and how he went about pleasing God, but I don't believe it is far-fetched to suppose he faced as many temptations and hindrances as any of us. Yet, somehow, he found a way to live and walk with God in such a way that his life became a pleasure to him.

HANOKH

We tend to gravitate to those that have gone before us and paved the way in how to do certain things well. Let's say I want to become a movie star. I might then study some of the best actors there are and learn from them in order to become as good as them or better. Well, I feel the same way about Enoch. He found the way to do what I have been seeking after. I am doing my best to know how he did it, but I am finding myself with more questions than answers. What did this man even like to do? Did he worship God all day long? Did he talk to him all the time, or just in the mornings or on his walks with him?

So I decided to look up his name in Hebrew and this is what I found: Enoch comes from the Hebrew word Hanokh, which means: dedicated, trained, or disciplined. I am quite excited about this finding because I can see all three descriptions being the perfect ingredients for winning a race. And not just any race, but a God pleasing one.

Some Christians seem to think becoming a Christ follower is all about loving Jesus and telling others about him. Well, I wish it was that simple. I have seen many leaders forget to take care of their own spiritual and physical needs, as well as that of their families. Sadly, they end up falling out of the race prematurely and even losing their loved ones as a result. I don't pretend to have all the answers, but I do believe going back to living a life of dedication, training and discipline can be keys to finishing our course strong.

I wonder what we would find if we were to ask church goers, or professing Christians, what their walk with God looks like on a daily basis. I think many would say their relationship with God is based on their church attendance. I recently heard the number of Christians who read the Bible is somewhere in the 10 percentile. The Bible is not an ordinary book. It is our major source for knowing God. It is how we learn to differentiate a lie from the Truth. And it is a key component in our relationship with our Creator, since it is He who chose to communicate with us through it. But just like running a race requires discipline and dedication, so does reading and meditating on God's Word.

The fact that you are reading this book tells me that you are hungry for more of God. There is something in you that must have sparked up when you read the title and then saw the possibility of going beyond a normal Christian life, to the one which has the possibility of pleasing our Creator.

The truth about Enoch who lived in the Old Testament times with no Bible or infilling of the Holy Spirit, no gift of tongues or salvation message, yet was able to live a life pleasing to God, should challenge us into going further with God. It is the highest calling there is. Our greatest example, Jesus, not only believed in it but lived it.

> *The one who sent me is with me; He has not left me alone, for I always do what **pleases** Him. (John 8:29 NIV)*

Prayer:

Father, I may not always get it right, but I purpose to follow in Jesus' footsteps and seek to always do what pleases you. Just like Enoch walked with you and pleased you, it is my heart's desire to live a life that is fully pleasing to you.

CHAPTER 5

Doesn't God know we could duplicate Enoch's success if He just gave us the details of his life? It would be a win–win situation where we learn the how-to's and He ends up with more God-pleasers. However, the more I think about it, the more I realize that having a manual and a checklist is not always the best idea. I for one enjoy making lists and checking them off. I get a great sense of accomplishment from them and if I am in need of extra self-worth, I can always challenge myself into getting things done in record time.

Of course, there is always the downside of a checklist, which happens when we are not able to check off all the boxes. It can produce the opposite effect and eventually plummet our sense of self worth. From experience I can say these same feelings of self worth, or lack thereof, tend to transfer into my walk with God. They either make me feel like I earned God's love, or worse, like I somehow displeased him.

GOOD WORKS

I wonder if this is part of the reason God chose not to give us more details on Enoch's life. If He had, would we follow them to the letter of the law? If so, wouldn't we be pleasing God through our own good deeds, instead of by his grace? And isn't this what the religious people of the Bible did? The very ones who crucified our Lord? Even Paul, when writing to the church in Ephesus lets us know we are destined to do good works, yet he first reminds us that of themselves, good works are not something to pursue:

> *For it was only through this wonderful grace that we believed in Him. Nothing we did could ever earn this salvation, for it was the gracious gift from God that brought us to Christ! So no one will ever be able to boast, for salvation is never a reward for good works or human striving. (Ephesians 2:8-9 TPT)*

When we read about David's life, we can readily see the good things he did, as much as the bad. We are shown his frailty as well as his great accomplishments. This makes him relatable in that he is imperfect just like us. And at the same time this is encouraging since he was called a man after God's own heart (1 Samuel 13:14). However, when it comes to following in Enoch's footsteps, we have some huge shoes to fill, yet we lack the knowledge of the ins and outs of his life.

Supposing Enoch's life was perfect, that he did everything just right, even checking off all the right boxes. In my experience, in trying to follow such a one, I would tend to strive in order to become perfect like him. Eventually this type of unrealistic expectation will only serve to show me my own human frailty. And instead of inspiring me to draw closer to God, it will eventually lead me to full discouragement and perhaps even hopelessness.

It is not that good works are bad in and of themselves or that we are to stay completely away from doing them. If this was so, Paul would not have told us to, "...work out your own salvation with fear and trembling" or that we are his workmanship, "created in Christ Jesus unto good works" (Philippians 2:12, Ephesians 2:10, KJV).

So what is it then? Do we get rid of all our checklists and focus only on spending time with God? Or do we put all our focus on working out our salvation with fear and trembling?

Many find themselves going from one extreme to the other. Unfortunately, we have all seen the results of either ditch. On the one hand, many Christians give the name of Jesus a bad reputation by the way they act. Things like honesty, hard work and being someone of good character are often lacking. On the other hand, when we try to please God based on our good works, it easily can turn into religion and undo Jesus' sacrifice on the cross.

> *If you want to be made holy by fulfilling the obligations of the law, you have cut off more than your flesh—you have cut yourselves off from the Anointed One and have fallen away from the revelation of grace! (Galatians 5:4 TPT)*

And we all know what that looks like. But what if it is neither/or, but both? What if we aim to live in a way worthy of him, yet fully aware it can only be through him?

A MATTER OF THE HEART

Isaiah 64:6 tells us that anything we do outside of Jesus, no matter how good of a thing it is, becomes like filthy rags in God's eyes. So if good works do not do the job, how can we please God?

> *But the Lord said to Samuel, "Do not look at his appearance or at his physical stature, because I have refused him. For the LORD does not see as man sees; for man looks at the outward appearance, but the LORD looks at the heart." (1 Samuel 16:7 NKJV)*

This verse is referring to the time when the prophet Samuel went to Jesse's house to anoint the next king of Israel. Jesse presented seven of his sons, all of which impressed Samuel, yet were turned down by God. It wasn't until David was brought in from the field that Samuel had God's approval to anoint him as Israel's future King. David then became God's fearless warrior who saved the day by killing Goliath and winning many battles against the Philistines. These are no small feats by any stretch of the imagination! The seemingly insignificant shepherd boy, whose own father did not consider him worthy of presenting to the prophet, became God's own hand-picked man.

Yet, in spite of David's great accomplishments, there is no denying he committed adultery, murder, and abuse of power. Nonetheless, God still speaks the following concerning him:

> *'I have found David the son of Jesse to be a man after my own heart, who will carry out all my will.' (Acts 13:22 CSB)*

Here is a man who was not concerned with checking-off the God pleaser's checklist, yet he is loved and chosen by God. In a nutshell, David's story reinforces the truth of our heavenly Father not looking for perfection or a sinless people. Instead, from the time Adam and Eve sinned, God had a plan of redemption in place. This plan of course is Jesus crucified for our sins.

In and through him, we are made righteous and able to please him. It is all through him! We can try and fool others, and sometimes even ourselves, but we can never fool God! He sees right through us. So, whether or not we do good works, what matters most to God is our hearts.

HEART INSPECTION

> *For in a visitation of the night you inspected my heart and refined my soul in fire until nothing vile was found in me. (Psalm 17:3 TPT)*

Notice in this Psalm David is not saying God is inspecting his deeds and evaluating whether he obeyed his commandments or not. God's testing of the heart has nothing to do with our good behavior or great deeds. It is all about the intentions of our heart. A great example of this is found in Saul and David's responses when they were each confronted with their sins.

In 1 Samuel chapters 13 and 15 we find Saul disobeying God's commands not once, but twice. The first time he did not wait for the prophet to arrive as he had been told to do and proceeded to offer the priestly sacrifice himself which was strictly forbidden (1 Samuel 10:8 and 13:8-9). The second time he chose to please the people and himself, rather than obey God (1 Samuel 15). Both times, when Samuel the prophet confronts him, Saul makes excuses for his disobedience. When he realizes Samuel is not budging, he begins to plead:

> *"I have sinned; but oh, at least honor me before the leaders and before my people by going with me to worship the Lord your God." (1 Samuel 15:30 TLB)*

Now, not only is Saul's heart not sorrowful before the Lord, but he separates himself from God by calling Him Samuel's God and not his own. I believe when we aim to please others and ourselves more than God, our hearts begin to harden towards God. And eventually, as in the case with Saul, we begin to draw away from him. In contrast, when David sins with Bathsheba and is confronted by the prophet, he sees his sin and becomes truly sorrowful before God:

> *It is against you and you alone I sinned, and did this terrible thing. You saw it all, and your sentence against me is just. You deserve honesty from the heart; yes, utter sincerity and truthfulness. Oh, give me this wisdom. Create in me a new, clean heart, O God, filled with clean thoughts and right desires. You don't want penance; if you did, how gladly I would do it! You aren't interested in offerings burned before you on the*

altar. It is a broken spirit you want—remorse and penitence. A broken and a contrite heart, O God, you will not ignore. And when my heart is right, then you will rejoice in the good that I do and in the bullocks I bring to sacrifice upon your altar. (Psalm 51:4, 6, 10, 16-17 and 19 TLB)

Both, Saul and David, were given similar opportunities to serve and please God. Both men were chosen and anointed by God to lead Israel. Both men disobeyed God and sinned. God sent them both prophets who confronted them for their sins. But this is where they both differed. One made excuses while the other took ownership for his actions. One shrugged off his disobedience as if it was not a big deal. The other prostrated himself before God with a true, repentant heart.

For the remainder of Saul's life, we don't see him wanting to please or follow after God. Instead, he lives a life of constant torment, fear and distrust. His unyielded heart spirals him down to even greater evil. With no reason other than jealousy, he makes his life's mission a pursuit to get rid of David, his faithful servant. In the process, he tries to kill his own son Jonathan, and massacres a whole town of innocent people, including 85 of God's priests (1 Samuel 22-24).

TESTED AND TRIED

The Lord God says, "I have made a solemn agreement with my chosen servant David. I have taken an oath to establish his descendants as kings forever on his throne, from now until eternity!" (Psalm 89:3-4 TLB)

Saul could have been that man, but through his actions, he chose not to be. David, on the other hand, pursued God with all of his might even when no one was looking, proving his personal love and commitment to God. There were no ulterior motives for him, just plain old fashion adoration for his King.

A crucible for silver, and a smelter for gold, and the LORD is the tester of hearts. (Proverbs 17:3 CSB)

I believe we are constantly given opportunities to be tested and tried. Many times these tests might not have anything to do with the present situation we are faced with. It could very well be God who sees the end from the beginning and is preparing us for an important assignment. As in the case of Abraham, when God asked him to sacrifice his son Isaac, He really did not intend for him to kill the son he waited so long for. Instead, God was testing him with what was most precious to him in order to fulfill his promise in making him the father of many nations (Genesis 17:5).

The LORD said, "Do not reach out [with the knife in] your hand against the boy, and do nothing to [harm] him; for now I know that you fear God [with reverence and profound respect], since you have not withheld from Me your son, your only son [of promise]." (Genesis 22:12 Amp)

Once more, God was looking for a lineage to pour his blessings through. From this test, Abraham became the Father of all of God's children, which also includes us! From that time on, God's people referred to God as: the God of Abraham, Isaac and Jacob. (ie: Moses in Exodus 3:6, 15, 16; 4:5.)

The more we seek to know God's heart, the more we realize He is not a hard task master or an unfair tester of hearts. He is clear with what He expects from us and makes his desires known. He is firm and just but always has our best in mind.

So when the Bible tells us David is a man after God's own heart, I believe its because he had been tested, tried and proven. David was not one to run away from tests, he actually requested them,

Search me, O God, and know my heart: try me, and know my thoughts. (Psalm 139:23 KJV)

Test me, LORD, and try me; examine my heart and mind.
(Psalm 26:2 CSB)

Our hearts represent the real us, our innermost thoughts, emotions and will; the deep part of us. Eventually what is in our hearts will come out through our actions, words and beliefs. However, most of the time we don't even know what is in our hearts and we end up doing things without understanding why. God alone knows our hearts and He is ever so gentle when we invite him to search them out. This is why David could ask God to test him without fear or hesitation. He trusted God's intention and character and truly wanted to please him.

Prayer:

God, I invite your searching gaze into my heart. Examine me through and through; find out anything that may be hidden within me. Whether in my heart or in my actions, show me if there is anything displeasing to you and help me make it right.

CHAPTER 6

Obedience is far better than sacrifice.
He is much more interested in your
listening to Him than in
your offering the fat of rams to Him

1 SAMUEL 15:22 TLB

In this story we find King Saul being given strict orders by the prophet Samuel to kill every living being which belonged to the Amalekites. In those days, the word of the prophet was the same as God's. However, when the prophet returns, he rebukes King Saul for choosing to keep what appealed to him and his men, rather than obeying God's instructions to destroy all. The Amplified version translates 'listening to him' as 'obedience to the voice of the LORD.' Interestingly enough, Saul assures Samuel he has obeyed him. So when Samuel asks him, "Then what is this sound of sheep, goats, and cattle I hear?" (1 Samuel 15:14 CSB), Saul responds:

> *"It's true that the army spared the best of the sheep and oxen," Saul admitted, "but they are going to sacrifice them to the Lord your God; and we have destroyed everything else."*
> *(1 Samuel 15:15 TLB)*

In a nutshell Saul disobeys, lies and justifies himself by twisting the truth. At the same time, he assumes he can appease God with the animal sacrifices and continue to be in his good graces. God is not impressed. It literally goes back to doing good works outside of God. Saul's sacrifices at this point would be considered filthy rags in God' sight. God does not need our sacrifices; what He desires is our heart. When He has our heart, it is evident in our obedience to him.

A few chapters later we find David in a very tight spot. He and his men were turned down from helping the Philistines fight Israel. After 3 days of traveling home, tired and disappointed, they found their camp had been burned down and their wives, children and animals carried away. In their distress, David's men speak of killing him (I Samuel 30). At this point, I am not sure things could get any worse for David. He's being constantly pursued by Saul and his men. He is rejected and not allowed to prove his faithfulness to the Philistines. He just lost his loved ones and all that he owned. And to top it all, the men he has led and trained are threatening to kill him.

Sometimes life feels that way, doesn't it? Just when we think we can't handle one more thing, something else jumps at us. Again, it is what we do in those moments, when we think we cannot go any further, and we are ready to throw in the towel, that matters most. Will we turn to God or to men? Will we give in to fear and despair or to faith and hope?

Although God knows what is in our hearts, we can read throughout the Bible how He likes to test his people. We can track it all the way back to Adam and Eve as they were tested through the tree of the knowledge of good and evil. This next scripture refers to the Israelites when they were tested:

> Remember that the LORD your God led you on the entire journey these forty years in the wilderness, so that He might humble you and *test you to know what was in your heart*, whether or not you would keep his commands. (Deuteronomy 8:2 CSB)

The bottom line is, God is most interested in our hearts! He will test us, not for his sake, but for ours. When Cain killed his brother Abel, God went to him and asked him where his brother was (Genesis 4:9-10). God, being all-knowing, was fully aware of what had happened. He was giving Cain a chance to come clean. I believe He does the same with us. He uses experiences, relationships and situations to reveal what is in our hearts. If we fail the test, He lovingly gives us opportunities to make it right. In Saul's case, he flunked the test and, sadly, also missed out on the opportunities to make it right.

In regards to Saul, God had clearly told him what to do with the Amalekites. The war was not the test. Instead, his obedience to God's instructions became his test. With David, it was not God causing Saul to pursue him, neither did He create the different calamities he was experiencing. However, I believe the test provided the opportunity to reveal how David would respond. Would he blame God or run to him for help?

As David's men spoke of stoning him, David was greatly distressed. Yet, the Bible tells us, "David encouraged himself in the LORD his God" (1 Samuel 30:6 KJV). In his dark hour of the night, David turned to the one, solid, constant in his life...God. No wonder God loved him, He knew he had David's heart. He had been pressed on all sides, yet in the end, I believe he came out more pleasing to God than the sacrifice of many animals.

THE SHEPHERD'S VOICE

All those years in the pastures as a shepherd boy, David learned to know God as his own Shepherd. So when hard times came, and they did, it was not unusual for him to run to him and to seek his voice. 1 Samuel 30 verse 8 tells us David inquired of the Lord for direction as to what to do next. He did not try to blame others or retaliate for their attacks. Neither did he consult them for what to do next. Instead, He went straight to God! In Him he found his strength, encouragement and much needed direction.

> *My own sheep will hear my voice and I know each one, and they will follow me. (John 10:27 TPT)*

Jesus calls himself the good Shepherd (John 10:11,14 and Hebrews 13:20). In Hebrews 13:5, He promises to never leave us or abandon us. And in the above verse, He refers to us as his sheep. These sheep know his voice and follow him. Moreover, throughout the Old and New Testament, we see many references concerning God as our Shepherd.

David got to live the life of a true shepherd. His early job consisted of caring for his father's sheep and he was very good at it. He made sure they were protected and that all intruders, such as the bear and the lion, were severely dealt with. While he was with the sheep day in and day out, David played his harp, mastered the slingshot and composed many songs to the lover of his soul, God. Reading the Book of Psalms is like getting a glance into his journal entries where we are privy to his raw and intimate conversations and thoughts with God. Whether as a young shepherd boy alone with his father's sheep, or a rich king surrounded by a crowd, David was not intimidated or embarrassed to praise and dance before his God. And even after desperate prayers, wounds and betrayals from friends, we see David in a constant state of contentment.

There is something so appealing about being with someone who is rooted deep in God. Someone who is not easily moved by circumstances or people, but whose trust is fully in their God. Just as Enoch, who habitually walked with God, so I believe, David continually talked and fellowshipped with him. He was a man who, much like Enoch, knew God and sought to please him! They were both men who chose to follow and obey God, rather than men.

Probably the most quoted Psalm in the Bible is Psalm 23, which begins with David declaring the Lord as his Shepherd. He describes his God as a Shepherd who took good care of him and who could be trusted, even while walking in the valley of the shadow of death. And as sheep look to their shepherd for guidance, so David learned to hear God's voice and to follow his leading from early on. This is why when he faced dire situations, it was normal for him to seek God first. People did not need to talk David into doing the things he did; feats such as dealing with the lion, the bear, and the giant. Instead, he faced them in complete trust and confidence in his God. This was not something he developed overnight. It was a lifestyle for him. It was what he chose to do day in and day out. I venture to say that David became dear to God's heart mostly from the habitual relationship he had cultivated alone in the pastures as a shepherd boy. That is where he learned to hear and obey his Shepherd's voice. And that is where we too, will learn to recognize our own Shepherd's voice.

BEING CLOSE TO HIM

Lord, who dares to dwell with you? Who presumes the privilege of being close to you, living next to you in your shining place of glory? Who are those who daily dwell in the life of the Holy Spirit? (Psalm 15:1 TPT)

As a mother, I relish the times any of my kids come to talk to me. Sometimes it might be about something funny that happened in their day, or something someone said to them that made them feel like a million bucks, or it could even be something hurtful that was bothering them. The fact that they choose to come to me, instead of any other person, means a lot to me. However, the fact that they have learned to trust me with their hearts is even more special.

Our relationships did not begin this way. It has been something we have built upon throughout the years. Nonetheless, the more we continue to grow our relationships, the greater our trust level grows and the closer we become.

As kids we tend to think life is all about "me." So as to be expected, I often find myself doing a lot of listening with each one. I learned to be content in their approach and desire to talk about themselves, and honestly, I really enjoy it! I love watching their expressions and seeing the lightbulb flash as they share their hearts. However, one of the most endearing things as a mother has been those moments when they stop to ask me about my day, about what is in my heart, or even my thoughts on something. I treasure the times when they put themselves aside and earnestly desire to know how I am doing. It brings our relationship to the next level. It somehow ceases to be a parent-child relationship, instead, it becomes one of friendship.

How much more does our heavenly Father enjoy when his kids approach him to talk and share their day with him. Or when they set aside their needs or personal burdens, to give him a hug and ask what is in his heart. We all have our own unique relationship with him, but how He must treasure our times when we put ourselves out of the way to just love on him. I can imagine as a parent that He loves it when we sit with him for no other reason than because we miss being with him.

Can you picture Enoch's life becoming so intimate with God that either he no longer belonged on the earth and God had to take him, or God just wanted him near 24/7? David, on the other hand, lived to be an old man, but was always fondly referred to as a man after God's own heart. Both men somehow learned to capture the longing of God's heart. Both men, I believe, took the time to earnestly seek to know the Father, and in doing so, they captured his heart.

> When I look up into the night skies and see the work of your fingers—the moon and the stars you have made—I cannot understand how you can bother with mere puny man, to pay any attention to him! (Psalm 8:3-4 TLB)

It completely undoes me to know that an all-sufficient God, who has everything He could ever want, desires to have an intimate relationship with us. It is beyond belief that the God of the universe, who knows everything about us, longs for fellowship with his children.

> His love broke open the way and he brought me into a beautiful broad place. He rescued me—because his delight is in me! (Psalm 18:19 TPT)

Prayer:

Father, I want to live next to you and commune daily with you. It is my heart's desire to see your face and be close enough to hear your heart beat for me. I love You!

CHAPTER 7

Here's the one thing I crave from God,
the one thing I seek above all else: I want
the privilege of living with Him every
moment in his house, finding the sweet
loveliness of his face, filled with awe,
delighting in his glory and grace. **I want to
live my life so close to Him**
that He takes pleasure in my every prayer

PSALM 27:4 TPT

noch and David were both men who found a way to tap into the very heart of God. Although it is true we do not have much information on Enoch, I believe David's life helps to fill in the gaps. For instance, in the Book of Acts we hear God say the following about David:

> *I have found in David, son of Jesse, a man who always pursues my heart and will accomplish all that I have destined him to do. (Acts 13:22 TPT)*

This is God expressing his own thoughts concerning David. And God, who knows all things, says it just as He sees it, "...a man who always pursues my heart." The Message Bible translates it this way:

> *"...He's a man whose heart beats to my heart..." (Acts 13:22 MESS)*

What does that even look like? Our hearts literally beating to God's own heart? Yet as extraordinary as this sounds, we are told David's heart did just that, so we must conclude that it is possible for us to do likewise. After seeing this, I no longer have as my ultimate goal to hear the Father say, "Well done my good and faithful servant;" based on how well I served Him here on earth. Instead, I am now challenged to walk at a deeper level. I want to be one who yearns to please God with the same measure as Enoch and David did.

I always thought being a man after God's own heart meant being a person with God's heart. One who thinks his thoughts, who cares for what He cares for and does his best to follow in his footsteps. And although this is partly true, I am now convinced there is another side to this verse.

This other side is that David was not only carrying God's heart for the people, but that he was always pursuing God's own heart. He pursued him for who He was, and not for what He could do for him. The Psalm above describes David craving to be next to God and being able to live with him. He was not satisfied in knowing about God, he wanted to sit next to him and see his beautiful face as he asked what was in his heart. David wanted the privilege of hearing his Creator's voice as they shared a heart-to-heart. Truly I believe that what separates David from most of us is his own approach towards God. David, a man after God's own heart, was consumed with desire for his Great Shepherd.

Have you ever been in a relationship where you felt used by the other person? You think you know someone, you give of yourself and hope it is reciprocated, only to find the relationship is one sided. I wonder how many times God encounters that same scenario. I wonder how many people who feel entitled approach him as if He is a genie and then forget to even thank him or visit with him until their next need.

I remember a time when I was teaching at the Bible school and in churches on a regular basis. I took time in God's presence, sought his face, read the Word, studied fervently, and sometimes even fasted in order to have a life-giving message for the people. I loved every bit of it, but as time went on, I noticed my personal relationship with my sweet Savior was being affected. Somewhere down the line, I began approaching God in order to pour into the people. I prioritized his calling over my life, instead of him. That is when I realized my heart was no longer beating after God's own heart, as it once had.

Eventually I began feeling depleted and unable to deal with my personal issues. I felt somewhat abandoned and used by the people and even by God. I was a young minister so it took me a while to understand the problem. In my own mind, I had done all that was asked of me and had given it my all to the ministry and the people. So it just did not make sense why I felt so empty and abandoned. Not until I began to understand that the problem was with me. I had somewhat walked away from my first love. Not that I did not love him, or had turned my back on him, but I had my priorities wrong.

I still sometimes find myself approaching the throne room with a huge list of concerns I want to petition God with. It is then I remember that having my needs met, or seeking him on behalf of others, is not as important as my relationship with him. Sometimes our cares seem like a huge mountain that blocks our view from everything else, yet it is in those moments that we must remember to put Jesus at the forefront. We must purpose to pursue his heart above all else and before all else.

From reading scriptures, it is so easy to see how God absolutely loves it when we approach him just because we love him and want to be with him.

It is amazing how often, when we take the time to love on our sweet Savior, that many of our needs or answers to our problems, get taken care of even before we ask. The same is to be said when talking to others about Jesus. As we prioritize him, ministering to them just flows effortlessly. It is from the very life we receive while we are in his presence that we are able to give to others. When reading Acts 13:22, I think it is safe to say that David was able to accomplish all that he was destined to do because he purposed to pursue God's own heart.

CRAVE

*O God of my life, I'm lovesick for you in this weary wilderness. I
thirst with the deepest longings to love you more, with cravings
in my heart that can't be described. Such yearning grips my
soul for you, my God! (Psalm 63:1 TPT)*

David craved to be in God's presence. His heart literally ached
for him. He yearned to be with God every moment of every day.
His longing was stronger than that of food or water.

*God, you are my God; I eagerly seek you. I thirst for you; my
body faints for you in a land that is dry, desolate, and without
water...So I gaze on you in the sanctuary...your faithful love
is better than life...You satisfy me as with rich food...When I
think of you as I lie on my bed, I meditate on you during the
night watches...(Psalm 63:1-6 CSB)*

There are many people with similar desires who will pray and ask
God for more of his presence, but then will leave it at that, waiting
for God to do something about it. It would be no different than a
person describing their desire to know us yet do nothing else
about it. If there is anything to be learned from David's life is that
he chased after God! He not only prayed and expressed his desire to
know God, but he pursued him with all of his might. David, who is
known for writing most of the Psalms, wrote them out of his deep
encounters with him. He was one who sought God before making
decisions and who worshiped him openly and without shame.

In the verses above, David compares his desire for God as
someone looking for water in the desert. I have been in a place of
such thirst that all I can think of is having a drink of water. At that
point, nothing else sounds good; not food, not even an ice-cold soda.
There are no substitutes for quenching that type of thirst. Your mind
and even your body begin to be affected by the lack of water. In fact,
dehydration is a bigger problem than we give it credit for. And this
is the kind of thirst David compares his longing for God to.

TASTE AND SEE

David was not a stranger to God's throne room. Much like Enoch, he was a regular. One can easily see how he was enamored with the LORD. When we read some of his Psalms, it is as if he is literally aching after God; anxiously waiting for his next meeting time with him. Some of the Psalms are like reading a gushy love letter in which a lover is begging the love of his life to live with him continually. He is longing for the chance to stare at their beauty, or even just spending time and enjoying their presence.

Through David, I can picture Enoch's conversation with God going something like this: "Please God, I beg you, let me stay with you longer. I cannot handle the thought of you letting me out of your sight. I know it's getting dark but could we just walk together some more?"

Taste and see that the LORD is good! (Psalm 34:8 CSB)

Both men, Enoch and David, had no doubt already tasted the goodness of the Lord. No longer could either one be persuaded to walk away from him. Nor could they see themselves continuing to live a plain, ordinary life void of passion and hunger for God. When most of us go to God for a few minutes here and there, these men longed to spend all of their time with him. They wanted to be in front of his face, so that when they spoke to him, it would always be from a place of intimacy.

I'm asking God for one thing, only one thing: to live with Him in his house my whole life long. I'll contemplate his beauty; I'll study at his feet. (Psalm 27:4 MESS)

After reading Psalm 27, along with many other Psalms penned by David, it is no wonder God was so pleased with him. This passionate man was not only interested in God's blessings, or in making it to heaven when he died, he actually longed for true intimacy with his Creator. And he would not settle for anything less.

The truth is once we taste of God's goodness, nothing else will do. Nothing can satisfy our thirsty souls like God alone can. Nothing will ever be able to fill the void we were created with, except for him; the One who formed us and knows us better than we know ourselves.

The Lord satisfies the longings of all his lovers... (Proverbs 10:3 TPT)

In David's case, he was just doing what was in his heart. He had enough of a relationship with God that he walked it out freely. His gratitude for God and excitement could not be contained. This is why he could take off dancing, shouting and removing his kingly clothes when worshiping his King (2 Samuel 6:14).

Sometimes we try too hard. As Christians, we can make it too complicated for ourselves and others to try and please our Father. Yet it's not a robotic, planned behavior that God is looking for. Far from it! Instead, He is eagerly hoping we will walk in the freedom Jesus has already provided for us. He is inviting us to enter into God's throne room. And He has already made a way for all of our needs to be met so that we can enjoy life to its fullness.

So now we come freely and boldly to where love is enthroned, to receive mercy's kiss and discover the grace we urgently need to strengthen us in our time of weakness." (Hebrews 4:16 TPT)

This may come as a shocker, but the reality is, life's pleasures were not meant for those who do not know God. They were meant for us, his children! When life happens, it should be LIFE HAPPENING! Our lives should be exciting! We should have fresh, new stories to tell our kids and grandkids. And they in turn should be motivated to explore all that God has for them.

GOD IS SEARCHING FOR...

*The Lord looks down in love, bending over heaven's balcony, looking over all of Adam's sons and daughters. He is looking to see if there is anyone who acts wisely, any who are **searching** for God and **wanting to please Him**. (Psalm 14:2 TPT)*

Do you realize God, the creator of all heaven and earth, is looking for those who are seeking for him? One of the Hebrew translations for the word "searching" means to frequent a place. God is not just looking for those who profess to love him, but for those who sincerely pursue him. Those who are in constant relationship with him.

As our creator, God has every right to demand our obedience and worship. Yet from the beginning of creation, He chose to give us free will. He gave us the option to follow him or reject him. And even after choosing him, through our free will, we get to choose whether or not we want to please him and pursue him with all our hearts.

If I was God, after wonderfully forming every human being, and giving them the option of becoming heirs with Jesus, I would be asking the following: "Is it too much to ask of you to come looking for me? To ask you to search for me and frequent my throne room? Is it unfair for me to wish you would want to spend time with me and please me?"

We were created to live in harmony with God our Creator. He did not create us to live separate from him. He is the source of all life. Apart from him we are spiritually dead. Even if we once knew him, but have walked away from him, we will look and search for answers and true fulfillment, but we will always come up wanting. We have all seen people who feel like they are missing out on life, or that God did them wrong, so they walk away from him in order to experience the world's bliss. Yet sooner or later, they realize it is all just a cheap counterfeit of the real.

God has made it so simple for us to know him, but somehow we go to painful extremes to try and fill the emptiness inside, outside of him. We are willing to pay whatever the cost, hoping we can find what we are looking for apart from him. Could it be that we just haven't had a real taste of his goodness? That we touched the water with our toes, but didn't jump all the way in? David makes it sound so easy:

> *Drink deeply of the pleasures of this God. Experience for yourself the joyous mercies He gives to all who turn to hide themselves in Him. Worship in awe and wonder, all you who've been made holy! For all who fear Him will feast with plenty. Even the strong and the wealthy grow weak and hungry, but those who passionately pursue the Lord will never lack any good thing. (Psalm 34:8-10 TPT)*

In hearing David's passion for God, it is as if a window into Enoch's own life is opened for us to see. He drank deeply into God's pleasures. He experienced for himself what it was like to hide ourselves in God. He learned to live in awe and wonder of his very own Creator. And as a result of his passionate pursuit of God, he too, never lacked any good thing.

When this type of exchange takes place, it is no longer us seeking to spend time with God, but He too is longing and looking forward to our times together. I believe it was a mutual longing for both Enoch and God. It became such that one day God had enough and said, "I am done with the formalities and proper processes of the human body. Enoch, how about you skip this whole death and funeral ordeal? From now on, let me keep you with Me."

> *...And Enoch walked with God: and he was not; for God took him. (Genesis 5:24 KJV)*

Prayer:

Dear God, I want to know and pursue you as Enoch and David did. I long to be in your presence and experience for myself your beauty and wonder. I want to drink deeply of your pleasures; to personally taste and see your goodness; and to desire you more than anything or anyone in this life.

CHAPTER 8

It is the glory of God to conceal a
thing: but the honor of kings is to
search out a matter

PROVERBS 25:2 KJV

S ometimes walking with God is similar to going on a treasure hunt. He seems to delight in putting out just enough bait to wet our appetites. I can picture a cartoon where a fresh baked pie is placed on a window sill to cool down. Next thing we see is a dog blindly following after the cloud of "pie-aroma." At first the smell is a little faint, yet enough to get its attention. Once he realizes there is something worth pursuing, he pulls out his sniffer and begins trailing after the wonderful scent. Shortly in his new pursuit, he notices that the closer he gets to a certain window, the stronger the smell becomes. He might not understand what it is he is after, except the fact that he cannot resist the smell and by now, whether due to curiosity or appetite, he will stop at nothing until he reaches its destination.

The same can be said about God reeling us in by setting out clues throughout our day to create hunger for him. It might be a song playing on the radio that touches our hearts, or a sweet word someone just shared with us. When things get a little hectic at work, we ask him for help and He fills us with his grace making everything better. By the time we get to the end of the list of clues, we can detect that his fingerprints are all over our lives. We begin blindly following his sweet aroma and outstretched arms.

We become like David, desperate for his presence. We begin pushing things out of the way, skipping unnecessary steps, and rushing to our destination, which is him! When we arrive, we close the door behind us and prostrate our faces before him. Oh, the joy of being with him. To be able to sit at his feet, rest our heads on his lap and tell him how much we love him, makes everything so complete!

When the Bible says not to cast our pearls among the swine (Matthew 7:6), I understand it to mean to not throw out what is precious to those who will not treasure it. Jesus himself spoke in parables so that his Truth would not be wasted on those who would not value it (Matthew 13:13). So honestly, I am not surprised to see Enoch's life written out as a special treasure in need of being found. It is written with just enough information to provoke us to hunger. However, unlike a real treasure hunt, God is not hiding himself to keep us from him...but to draw us to him!

Do you ever wonder why God likes to "hide" things from us? Wouldn't life be so much simpler if He just tells us things that help fulfill his will on earth, without us having to ask, seek or knock? The Scripture above says He likes to conceal things and that it is our honor to search or investigate them out. In answer to this question, it is my belief that God too likes to be pursued. He likes it when He sees his children seeking and following after him.

DEDICATED

Although we don't have many of the nitty-gritty details in Enoch's life, it does us well to look at the clues that we have been privy to. For instance, knowing the importance God gives to names throughout the Old and New Testament, let's revisit from a previous chapter, the meaning of Enoch's name:

Enoch's name: to dedicate; disciplined; or consecrate.

According to the "Expository Dictionary of Bible Words," the underlying idea of this name seems to be one of initiation. Especially in the Old Testament, it focuses on ceremonies that inaugurate the use of something for God's service, a devoted cause, or given over to a particular purpose. It is to be set apart for God's special use or to be holy.

So what exactly does it mean to be holy or set apart? It is to be removed from the realm of the common into the sphere of the sacred. Therefore, to be holy is a technical term used for persons, places, times, and things that are considered sacred due to their association and consecration to God. For example, the 7th day is considered holy, to be reserved for worship and rest (Genesis 2:3; Exodus 20:8-11; Deuteronomy 5:12), the same could be said of Mt. Sinai (Exodus 19:23), of the priests of Israel (Leviticus 21:7), and even Israel itself, which was chosen and set apart by God as his own special possession (Deuteronomy 7:6; 14:2, 21).

GOD'S SPECIAL POSSESSION

Can you imagine being chosen to be God's special possession by no other than God himself? Peter says it this way:

> But you are a chosen people, a royal priesthood, a holy nation, God's special possession, that you may declare the praises of Him who called you out of darkness into his wonderful light. (1 Peter 2:9 NIV)

When I was a little girl, one of my favorite possessions was a light blue toy suitcase. It had a small white handle, two plastic locks, and was no bigger than a large, thick book. I took my little suitcase with me everywhere I went. It was little, but it carried all the essentials I considered important in my life. And the neat thing about it was that I got to pick what I put in it. It was without a doubt my special possession!

My mom tells me of a time when we were visiting some of their friends. After a day or two, the lady of the house became very suspicious of my little suitcase. I suppose she thought I was stealing things since I never put it down or went anywhere without it. Thankfully my dear mom caught on to it and to appease the lady's fears, she had me open it to display the array of all the wonderful things I carried in it.

On another occasion, I was told we were crossing a very busy intersection in Mexico City. Back then its population was around eighteen million people and some of the streets had as many as eight lanes going one way. As we were hurrying to cross one of those busy intersections, I dropped my little blue suitcase and it popped open. I can only imagine the embarrassment I put my parents through as a hundred plus items went bouncing all over the pavement holding up traffic. Worse yet, was the fact I refused to leave without my special possessions. I am told different pedestrians and cars stopped to help me pick up the items. We now talk and laugh about it; but the truth is, I was so taken with this little suitcase that I literally exposed my family and others to danger and embarrassment because of it.

What was in it that was so important? Well, I did not remember that part, so I called my mom to ask her about it and this is what she said, "You had all the little salt and pepper shakers, little packages of saltine crackers, and coffee stirring straws from the airplanes, as well as the tiny soaps, small shampoo and conditioner bottles from the hotels." As she revealed this, we both laughed so hard! After a good laugh, I came to my senses and I asked mom again, "Do you mean to tell me all of those people in Mexico City put their lives on the line for free plastic salt and pepper shakers?" She confirmed I did.

We are God's special possession! Regardless of what we look like or what we do, we are his special treasure. We don't have to be the best or the most popular for him to choose us. We just need to choose to follow him!

In Exodus 19:5-6 and Malachi 3:17, the word possession comes from the Hebrew word segulla, which means a special treasure. The foot note in "The Passion Translation" says the following: "It is used to describe "guarded wealth," indicating the placement of the king's jewels, treasures, etc., in a safe, protected place because of their extraordinary value. God says that each believer is a priest and king, his unique and special treasure of great importance—a treasure above all other treasures."

HIS OWN

In the New Testament, Titus explains the purpose for the crucifixion: redemption, freedom from wickedness, and...

> *...to purify for Himself a chosen and very special people to be His own possession, who are enthusiastic for doing what is good. (Titus 2:14 AMP)*

The Passion Translation reads, "...He claims you as his very own." The emphasis here is on: "his own." So not only are we God's special treasure, his guarded wealth for whom He died, we are his very own possession! He bought and paid for us in full. God himself calls us his special possession.

> *Indeed, I have inscribed [a picture of] you on the palms of My hands... (Isaiah 49:16 AMP)*

We are his people that are called by his Name. We are ever before him. He is constantly thinking of us! And according to this verse, He has us tattooed on the palm of his hands.

PASSIONATE TO DO

> *He sacrificed himself for us that He might purchase our freedom from every lawless deed and to purify for himself a people who are his very own, passionate to do what is beautiful in his eyes. (Titus 2:14 TPT)*

Do you realize that pleasing God is actually his idea? Not only has He purchased our freedom and made a way for us to be righteous before him, but He is seeking a people who are passionate to do what is pleasing to him.

When we see God's heart for us, and get to know and experience his desire for us, Christianity ceases to be a set of rules under the guise of religion. Instead, it becomes a joy and a privilege to do what is beautiful in his eyes. We begin to live, move, and have our being from a relationship with a God who unconditionally loves us. It is this same God who has won our hearts over and over with his immeasurable love for us. It is easy now to see why David could unashamedly proclaim his love and passion for him, and why Enoch chose to walk and please God all the days of his life.

So just as Enoch was dedicated for God's purpose and glory, we get to choose whether or not we live a life of consecration to him. It is up to us how far we run with it. We are called his special possession. Will we follow his loving aroma to its full destination, or will we turn back and continue our human, basic paths? My heart feels overwhelmed in knowing that the Creator of the whole universe wants me! That He has a particular purpose and destiny for my life for which He is giving me the opportunity and honor to consecrate myself for.

Prayer:

Jesus, wow, you did it all for me! You sacrificed yourself for my freedom, so I could choose you. You called me your special possession, so I could please you. I say, yes Lord, use me! Yes Lord, take me as your very own. I consecrate myself to you to be a pleasing aroma of delight.

CHAPTER 9

The appetite of a worker works for him,
for his **hunger** urges him on

PROVERBS 16:26 AMP

What are we hungry for? Where is our appetite taking us? Everyone is hungry for something. For some it may be having our basic needs met, such as food and water. For others it could be fame, riches, success. What is it that drives us? Or as the above proverb says, what is urging us on?

Most people can probably agree that having our needs met is important and that the feeling of appreciation and success is nice. However, there is more to hunger than meets the eye. Jesus, our perfect example, went about doing good everywhere He went. But I wonder, what did He hunger after? Did He have an appetite beyond food and healing the sick? If so, what was it? Perhaps John's account of the time Jesus met the woman at the well will help us understand him in this area:

> Wearied by his long journey, He sat on the edge of Jacob's well. He sent his disciples into the village to buy food, for it was already afternoon. Soon a Samaritan woman came to draw water. Jesus said to her, "Give me a drink of water." ...the disciples returned and were stunned to see Jesus speaking with the Samaritan woman ... Then the disciples began to insist that Jesus eat some of the food they brought back from the

village, saying, "Teacher, You must eat something." But Jesus told them, "Don't worry about me. I have eaten a meal you don't know about." (John 4:6-8, 27, 31-32 TPT)

Jesus and his disciples had been ministering to the people of Judea and were now on their way to Galilee. After walking under the hot sun, Jesus was tired, hungry and thirsty. He stopped to sit at Jacob's well in Sychar while his disciples went into the village to buy food. When they return and Jesus rejects their food, the disciples begin wondering who fed him. To this Jesus responds:

"My food is to be doing the will of Him who sent me and bring it to completion." (John 4:34 TPT)

Just a little bit earlier, Jesus had been so tired, He chose to sit and wait for them to bring him food. On their return, his disciples found him talking away with a Samaritan woman and claiming He had already eaten. What they did not realize is, that while they were gone, Jesus set aside his need for physical nourishment and used it instead, to minister to a woman whom most Jewish people would have avoided. (Not only was she a Samaritan woman, but she had also been married and divorced 5 times and was living with a man whom she was not married to.) As a result of their conversation, the woman ended up believing in Jesus and evangelizing her whole town.

I find this story to be a wonderful illustration of what it looks like to walk in God's Kingdom perspective. Jesus' hunger to do his Father's will was stronger than meeting his physical needs. Consequently, He was no longer hungry for natural food, rather his need for food, water and rest were taken care of when He followed his Father's will.

There is no denying that as long as we live in this body, we have physical needs that are real, and sometimes very loud. Yet there is a greater appetite to be met. I believe this supernatural hunger is not just for Jesus. We, too, can live above our natural appetites in a higher reality where pleasing God becomes more important and rewarding.

THE KINGDOM OF HEAVEN

When we read the Gospels, we often see Jesus stopping to teach his disciples about the Kingdom of Heaven. He frequently took things, which were familiar to the people, and used them to illustrate a Kingdom reality. Most of his parables began with, "The Kingdom of Heaven is like..." (ie: a mustard seed, a fisherman, a hidden treasure, etc.) The people understood what He was talking about and those who wanted to know the unseen world of God could do so through his teachings.

We can often miss God's Kingdom realities by trying to spiritualize the Truth. Clearly, God created us knowing that it would be hard to understand the unseen realm of the Spirit through our physical bodies and five senses. Therefore, it was his idea from the beginning, to use the things in this world to help us understand him and his Kingdom better.

> For ever since the creation of the world His invisible attributes, His eternal power and divine nature, have been clearly seen, being understood through His workmanship [all His creation, the wonderful things that He has made], so that they [who fail to believe and trust in Him] are without excuse and without defense. (Romans 1:20 AMP)

Therefore, it must go without saying, that when Jesus tells his disciples his food is doing the will of the Father, He was helping them and us understand what it is like to obey God through a natural, bodily need. As our minds begin to expand with the Truth of God's Word, we become more spiritually focused and conscientious. In other words, the more time we spend reading and meditating on his Word, the more heaven minded we become. And when we add the baptism of the Holy Spirit and pray in our heavenly language (speaking in tongues), we become a powerhouse (Acts 2:4; Mark 16:17; 1 Corinthians 14:2,4). Eventually, walking in his will begins to take preeminence over our own desires. This is when his Kingdom reality supersedes our appetites.

When we read that Enoch walked with God, and somewhere in that process he pleased him, it helps me realize that walking with God and hungering after him is not as complicated as we might think. On the contrary, it is really so simple...but it does require prioritizing him.

Going back to my original question in this chapter, what are we hungry for? Is it to satisfy our fleshly desires and needs? Or can we move beyond them and replace our appetite with God's desires?

APPETITE

I know sometimes we have to fan the flames of hunger. For some, having spiritual hunger can sound foreign or be nonexistent. My first appreciation for this word and its counterpart, appetite, was during a time when my mom was diagnosed with cirrhosis of the liver and placed on a transplant list for nearly 3 years. By then, she was bedridden and her body had whittled down to skin and bones.

As you can imagine, having the right nutrients was imperative to keeping her alive while she waited for a new liver. Unfortunately, she had zero appetite, so the task of nourishing her was not an easy one. I remember a certain day when my brother kept going back and forth from the kitchen to where my mom's room was in the basement. After watching this take place a few times, I decided to go and investigate. It turns out, my dear brother, not being an expert on how mom liked her eggs, kept making them. Unfortunately, they were turned down each time. Without an appetite, my mom required the eggs to be made perfectly to her liking to even touch them. This meant my brother ended up cooking and eating 4 to 5 eggs before he made one she would eat.

This incident always stuck with me, because until then, I had not realized how important it is to have an appetite. In this case, my mom not having one, made her an extremely picky eater. Her body needed food and nutrients desperately. So had my dad or brother not persisted in getting the food just right, it could have resulted in her dying of starvation.

We are told to put our eyes on things above, where God is, and not on earthly things (Colossians 3:2). Yet, without an appetite for the things of God, it would be hard, if not impossible, to move towards pleasing him. Sometimes we can be in a state much like my mom's without an appetite, which can lead us to spiritual malnutrition, and in some cases even death. This is why it is vital to fan the flames of hunger for God.

THE BREAD OF LIFE

How do we fan those flames? How do we go from having no appetite for pleasing God, to being driven with the hunger to do so? We must remember that we are spirit beings created in God's own image. Our bodies are not the real us, they are just the earthly suits we live in. We also have a soul, which consists of our mind, our will and our emotions. With that in mind, just as eating regular food nourishes and keeps our physical bodies alive, so eating spiritual food does for our spirits. In the above scriptures, when Jesus declares his food is to do the will of the Father, it is evidence that his earthly appetites were dominated by his spiritual ones. In another scripture we read:

> *"Man must not live on bread alone but on every word that comes from the mouth of God." (Matthew 4:4 CSB)*

God's Word is food to our beings; it satisfies our souls; and heals our bodies. It is a complete, powerful, super food!

> *"I am the bread of life," Jesus told them. "No one who comes to me will ever be hungry, and no one who believes in me will ever be thirsty again...The one who eats my flesh and drinks my blood has eternal life, and I will raise him up on the last day,*

because my flesh is true food and my blood is true drink..."
(John 6:35 and 54-55 CSB)

Certainly Jesus did not mean we are to eat his physical flesh and drink of his blood in order to have eternal life, did He? No, that would be physically impossible for us to do. Instead, Jesus is teaching us a spiritual, kingdom reality through a physical illustration. He is speaking in a language anyone, no matter the culture or age, can relate to. The message is clear: Jesus alone can give us eternal life and we are to hunger and thirst for Him as we are for real food and drink.

In the same way that nursing infants cry for milk, you must intensely crave the pure spiritual milk of God's Word. For this 'milk' will cause you to grow into maturity, fully nourished and strong for life-especially now that you have had a taste of the goodness of the Lord Jehovah and have experienced his kindness. (1 Peter 2:2-4 TPT)

It is no secret that we crave whatever we feed on! Our appetites follow the things we spend our time, effort, and attention on. So it is with pretty much everything around us: music, food, entertainment, talents, appearances, etc. If you want to be more of something, submerge yourselves in it. Especially when it comes to loving our beautiful Savior. If we find ourselves not hungry enough to want to please our King, let's saturate ourselves with him. That includes more of his presence, his Word, his Spirit, his people, etc. I love how Peter puts it in the prior verse, 'intensely crave.' What happens when we crave God's Word as much as a baby craves milk? We will be fed. May we feel that same intensity until nothing else satisfies us.

Something else that has helped fan in me a hunger for more of God is reading the lives of great men and women of old who lived and saw God do amazing miracles, signs and wonders throughout their lives. Men and women such as: Smith Wigglesworth, Amy Semple McPherson, Kathryn Kuhlman, and Charles Finney, among so many others. Their surrendered, sold out lives and testimonies stir me to want a deeper, consecrated life to God. They leave me hungering for more of him and of his power in my life. They saw legs grow, tumors disappear, eyes form from nothing. With some, such as in the case of Finney, even whole towns turned to Jesus with bars and theaters closing their doors because no one went to them anymore. What is also exciting is knowing that God is not a respecter of persons (Acts 10:34). What He did for them, He can and wants to do through us. So, let us not stop now, but let us move on by saturating ourselves with the right spiritual food.

WORK

"Don't work for the food that perishes but for the food that lasts for eternal life, which the Son of Man will give you..." (John 6:27 CSB)

No one said it would be easy, for nothing worth having ever is. It is going to require work on our part. But as in the example of Jacob who was willing to work for 14 years for Rachel, the Bible says:

...and they seemed like only a few days to him because of his love for her. (Genesis 29:20 CSB)

When our desire to please God comes from our love for him, doing his will can seem like a walk in the park, just as it was for Jacob. He must have worked hard during those years, but his love for Rachel was stronger than his physical demands. So it is when we follow after the Father from the deep longings of our heart, doing his will ceases to become a chore or a list of do's and don'ts. What was once a form of a religion begins to turn into a relationship.

Where do we start? Well, let's begin with reading the Bible, which is our sure foundation. How about reading 10 chapters a day? or 10 pages? or even 10 minutes? At first, there might not be any 'aha' or 'wow' moments, but the more we do it, the more it will begin to transform our appetites. It's much like going on a green healthy diet. It can be hard at first, especially if you are not used to eating healthy food. Your body might want to kick, scream and have withdrawals. Before you know it, your body will stop craving junk or processed food, and begin hungering after what is good and healthy. Eventually you won't even need to tell your body to stay away from those delicious, freshly made, warm brownies. You might take a bite and realize you no longer like it.

> *Open my eyes to see the miracle-wonders hidden in your word. I am continually consumed by these irresistible longings, these cravings to obey your every commandment! (Psalm 119:18, 20 TPT)*

On a personal note, I have found that my best times reading the Bible have been those when I take the time to ask the Holy Spirit to join me. I pray something as simple as this, "Holy Spirit, would you please come read with me and speak to me?" I also like to ask him questions, such as: "What does this mean? Holy Spirit, what is really going on here? Will you please explain this? Or, what are you trying to say to me?"

EXCEED OUR WILDEST IMAGINATION

As we become part of God's great army for these end times, we must first become a people who are sold out and in pursuit of him. With that in mind, there is so much our Commander in Chief has for us. He wants to fill us up and equip us in every possible way. Paul understood this well and therefore wrote to the Ephesian Church some of the most wonderful revelations about our heavenly Father's desire towards us:

> *Every spiritual blessing in the heavenly realm has already been lavished upon us as a love gift from our wonderful heavenly Father...I pray that he would unveil within you the unlimited riches of his glory and favor until supernatural*

strength floods your innermost being with his divine might and explosive power....this extravagant love pours into you until you are filled to overflowing with the fullness of God!... He will achieve infinitely more than your greatest request, your most unbelievable dream, and exceed your wildest imagination! He will outdo them all, for his miraculous power constantly energizes you. (Ephesians 1:3, 3:16, 19-20 TPT)

What if all along, God has been waiting for us in order to fulfill our hunger and desire for more of him? I have read and prayed Paul's prayers to the Ephesians for years, but it has just now occurred to me to consider the following: What if verse 20, of chapter 3, is meant in the area of hungering after God? I believe He wants to give us a desire and hunger for him infinitely more than our "... greatest request, our most unbelievable dream and exceed our wildest imagination." What if He outdoes them all?

It is very possible that for most of us, our appetites need a whole revamping. They may need to be awakened, fanned, and restored to their original design. Any desire we have towards God comes from him...deep calls unto deep. Therefore, our part in this is to begin by asking him for it. He has it, we want it. He wants to give it to us, we ask and pursue him for it.

Ask, and it will be given to you; seek, and you will find; knock, and it will be opened to you. For everyone who asks receives, and he who seeks finds, and to him who knocks it will be opened. (Matthew 7:7-8 NKJV)

Prayer:

Dear Lord, I am so done with being complacent in my relationship with You. The truth is, I long for your presence! I am so hungry to know You more and to please You with every part of me. I want to be saturated with You my King. My request, my prayer, is to have more of You! To have your presence become my greatest need. Thank you Lord!

CHAPTER 10

So whether we live or die we make
it **our life's passion** to
live our lives pleasing to Him

2 CORINTHIANS 5:9 TPT

W hat would our lives look like if, like Enoch, our sole ambition was to please the Father? Can you imagine being at the same place Paul was when he wrote this verse? I don't believe he was trying to impress the church at Corinth with poetic and pious sounding words. I believe rather, he was nonchalantly expressing his present state with God.

In the prior verse, after stating his desire to be in heaven, Paul goes on to declare that no matter whether he was in heaven or on earth, all his life's ambitions were narrowed into one: to please God! He was sold out to God and did not care what was done to him or how close he came to dying. Even when being warned of trouble ahead, although he had plenty of opportunity, he did not look for the easy way out. Instead, it appears as if he did everything possible to speed up his trip to heaven. At one time, the people pleaded with him not to go to Jerusalem due to various prophetic warnings, yet this was his reply:

> *"What are you doing, weeping and breaking my heart? For I
> am ready not only to be bound but also to die in Jerusalem for
> the name of the Lord Jesus." (Acts 21:13 CSB)*

I find it interesting that those who warned Paul not to go to Jerusalem were people who knew how to hear from God and who spoke by his Spirit. So if the warnings were from God, why then would Paul not obey? Could it be that maybe he had a choice in the matter and God was using it to see how much he was willing to suffer for him? To see how far he was willing to please him?

It is no surprise that the enemy hated Paul and tried to get rid of him in every way he could. Since he wasn't able to discourage him, kill him, or persuade him to look out for himself, he ended up putting him in prison, hoping that would give him the least amount of influence. But you see, when our lives are pleasing to the Father, it does not matter what happens to us, because God is able to turn it all around for our good and for his glory.

> *So we are convinced that every detail of our lives is continually woven together to fit into God's perfect plan of bringing good into our lives, for we are his lovers who have been called to fulfill his designed purpose. (Romans 8:28 TPT)*

BE STILL

What the enemy meant for evil, God turns for good. Such is the case with Paul's imprisonment. The enemy meant to silence him; instead, the silence provided an opportunity for Paul to write almost half of the epistles. I'm sure the devil still wishes he had never imprisoned Paul. Just think, it is through his imprisonment that Paul was able to help the churches in Ephesus, Philippi, and Colossae, as well as his friend Philemon. Furthermore, the revelation in his letters, which was foundational for the early Church, continues to instruct and transform untold billions today. This might not have taken place if he had kept to his busy schedule and not been forced into a quiet time to reflect and seek God for greater insight.

Can you imagine being in a cell day in and day out for days without end? Whether you have others in your cell or it's just you, there is nothing but time to pass by. You can't just get up and go somewhere when you want to, nor pick up your phone and talk the day away. Sooner than later, you will find yourself having a lot of time to think and reflect on what is most important.

Be still, and know that I am God... (Psalm 46:10 KJV)

These two words, 'be still,' can be translated from the Hebrew to mean: relax, withdraw or be quiet. And from the English it is often defined as: without movement, free from sound or noise, peaceful or calm.

As in Paul's example above, sometimes we are forced into a place of withdrawal and void of movement and sound, but many times we have to choose to separate ourselves to be still before God Almighty.

Recently, after what felt like a busy day, I went to bed feeling at odds with myself and my surroundings. I felt overwhelmed and unsettled. As I tossed and turned for over an hour, I decided to get up and move into the living room. I sat my computer aside, feeling the need to just sit still. That is when it dawned on me the reason I felt so at odds. If I were to define it into one word, it would be "business" (although the Bible might describe it as the "cares of this world").

I needed my quiet time with God. I felt so distant. I had read my Bible and prayed, yet by the end of the day, after having people and constant activity, I just needed to be still and know that He is God!

As I sat on my couch with the lights still off, I asked the Father if I could just sit with him. It wasn't but a few minutes of laying by his side, with his arm across my shoulders, that I began feeling so complete. That is truly all I needed...to be still and know that He is God. Oh the joy of silence! When we invite God into it, it is truly medicine to our souls.

BESIDE QUIET WATERS

Something happens in the stillness of time when we separate ourselves from the noise, the busyness and the distractions that are all around us in order to be quiet before our Father. It is healing, therapeutic and so needed. It is where we find God and get to know who He really is. It is where we can experience his presence and goodness to us.

He lets me lie down in green pastures; He leads me beside the still and quiet waters. He refreshes and restores my soul (life)... (Psalm 23:2-3 AMP)

Throughout the Bible, we see people do great exploits for God; people like Moses, Joseph and David, to name a few. Yet before they parted the sea, saved a nation from starvation, or killed a giant with a single stone, they were people who knew God in their private and alone times...in their prayer closet. The truth is, we cannot claim to know God in public if we have not first taken the time to know him in private.

If the Bible had been written under our present culture, I have to believe that the command to be still or silent would come up a lot more often. In today's modern culture, which prides itself in being busy, it is hard not to have our minds constantly working and cluttered with things. We are glued to screens of all sizes and shapes. If that is not enough, we have places to go, people to see, jobs to do, and entertainment to be had. So something that in Bible times would have seemed normal, such as carving a few minutes out of a day to sit and to be still, is very challenging for an average person. For example, have you ever tried laying on your back with your feet up on a chair and your arms by your side for 15 short minutes in total silence? I did it, and I have to confess that it was one of the longest 15 minutes of my life. As a matter of fact, the first time I tried it, I could not even finish the allotted time.

Unfortunately, not being used to silence or stillness affects our relationship with God. It is often hard for us to make time to be quiet before him. I know for me, I can think of many things that need to be done before I can stop to say good morning to my Father. Many times I have to speak to my thoughts and bring them under submission to the obedience of Christ. I literally quote 2 Corinthians 10:5 until my mind settles down and I can focus on the One who is worthy of all my attention.

Where did David learn to know God? Certainly not in the war line while the Philistines taunted the Israelites with Goliath and definitely not in the busy courtroom as King of Israel. No, it was way back in the green pastures, by the quiet waters, where he spent his days and nights taking care of his father's sheep. Without many distractions or people to talk to, it was just him and God. Much like Enoch on his walks with God and Paul in the prison cell, David got to hear God's whispers and learned to know God's heart. He sat and played his harp, he talked and walked with God, he stopped and listened to his voice. As a result, he too received many revelations which still move us today. One such is this following Psalm:

> *God's splendor is a tale that is told; His testament is written in the stars. Space itself speaks His story every day through the marvels of the heavens. His truth is on tour in the starry vault of the sky...Each day gushes out its message to the next, night with night whispering its knowledge to all. Without a sound, without a word, without a voice being heard. Yet all the world can see its story... (Psalm 19:1-4 TPT)*

At the beginning of the year, our youngest son and I set out to memorize Psalm 23. Around that time, there was an afternoon where my thoughts kept racing around and my mind wouldn't calm down. When I asked God for help, I felt as if He was inviting me to go to a stream of water. Knowing there wasn't one near, I knew He was asking me to do it through the eyes of my mind where my thoughts were still racing. As I closed my eyes and pictured a brook, this stream that appeared in my imagination was anything but quiet.

There was so much water rushing through the stream that it sounded loud and fast, much like my thoughts. So in my mind, I moved upstream a bit where it seemed less pressured and a little quieter, but not quiet enough. Once again, I moved further up and soon found I could hardly hear the water moving. As I looked closer, I noticed there was just enough movement to let the water through the stream making a most soothing sound. It did not take long for the quiet and gentle brook to begin refreshing me. So there I sat by this soothing stream, until I felt so calm that I nearly fell asleep.

IN CONSTANT TOUCH WITH GOD

Enoch...when he was 365, and in constant touch with God, he disappeared, for God took him! (Genesis 5:22 TLB).

One of God's old generals, Smith Wigglesworth, was once asked how long he prayed. He responded by saying he didn't pray for more than fifteen minutes at a time, but that he also did not go for more than fifteen minutes without praying. This man, no doubt, knew God and was in constant communion with him.

For one such as Enoch, who was in constant touch with God, could mean that his walks with God eventually were not enough. I believe that from the moment he woke up until the time he went to bed, he must have talked and fellowshipped with God. It had to be a constant interaction between the two. And maybe even as he slept, God spoke to Enoch in dreams or through the quietness of the night. It is evident, however, that they both loved being with each other, so much so, that Enoch was transported to heaven without ever experiencing death.

Eventually, our times together with our Father can become so rich, we no longer want to leave his presence. We just want to be with him. Can you imagine getting to the place where it literally hurts to leave our prayer closet in order to tend to our daily responsibilities?

MY BELOVED-MY FRIEND

Some believe the Book of Song of Songs gives us a glimpse into Jesus' passionate heart for his bride. Whether that is so or not, it is no mystery that through the Shulammite woman we can see the account of a bride-to-be who is madly in love with her future husband and vice-versa. This book is like a love poem in which both man and woman are equally matched in their love and desire for each other. Here is a small excerpt of her account:

> *Most sweet are his kisses, even his whispers of love. He is delightful in every way and perfect from every viewpoint. If you ask me why I love Him so, O brides-to-be, it's because there is none like Him to me. Everything about Him fills me with holy desire! And now He is my beloved-my friend forever. (Song of Songs 5:16 TPT)*

In the last 7 verses of chapter 5, the Shulammite woman describes her beloved in a manner to make one think he is an otherworldly being; a god of some sort. First she says he is exquisitely handsome and outstanding among 10 thousand men. She then describes his head as of pure gold and his hair like clusters of dates and black as ravens. From there she depicts his eyes, his cheeks, his lips, his hands, his abdomen, his legs, his appearance, and lastly, his kisses. Of course, by the time she comes to the end, she can't help but say that he is perfect in every way. To her, no other man can compare or come close to him, making it evident to all that she finds him most delightful and desirable.

It is no secret that the more time we spend with someone, the more our relationship grows in closeness. As we place our focus on them and begin uncovering the secrets of their heart, it becomes like an unexplainable addiction where we just can't get enough of them.

The Shulammite's account speaks of a person who has taken the time to be with someone she deeply cares for. She studies him in every possible way, pondering upon his whole being. She probably lays awake at night trying to figure out what every part of him resembles; and then, more than likely, she walks through her day longing for another chance to be with him. She is mesmerized by him. Her gaze, her time and her thoughts are only for him.

By now, it must be concluded that the Shulammite woman is a total mess. She can hardly sleep, talk, or give her full attention to those around her or her chores at hand. It is all meaningless without him. The sole essence of her life has been narrowed down to that of pleasing him! No longer is she enticed by other goals or life's achievements. They all become futile and pale in comparison. She now joins Solomon in saying, "Vanity, vanity, all is vanity."

NONE LIKE HIM

So whether we live or die we make it our life's passion to live our lives pleasing to Him. (2 Corinthians 5:9 TPT)

What if we were the Shulammite woman and Jesus was our lover? Can you picture missing him so much that we sit at his feet for hours just to feel his nearness? What if someone asked us to describe our lover, what would we say?

I am told that when my mom was a little girl of 4 or 5 years of age, she began skipping school. After several days of missing school, my grandmother received a shocking call concerning her daughter's absence. It was then discovered that every morning, as mom was supposed to walk to school, instead she became captivated by a certain handsome business man that lived between her house and the school. It became her custom to set herself outside one of his windows and simply delight her eyes by staring at the man. And she did this for hours until it was time to go home.

As I sit here writing about this story, I am convicted of the fact that I can hardly sit in silence at my Savior's feet without getting antsy or thinking of the dozen things I should be doing. Many times I end up leaving his presence prematurely. Yet, a little girl of no more than

5 years of age could stand for hours just staring at a person without a care or a need to rush away.

Maybe all we know about Jesus physically is that he has piercings in his hands and in his feet. But I wonder, what if we are determined to gaze into his beautiful face and linger long enough to notice the color of his eyes? Would we be able to look deep into them and feel his love come surging out? Can you imagine studying Jesus' face, his demeanor, his personality, his likes and dislikes, etc., in order to please him better? What if we did it as if our lives depended on it? As if it became our greatest need?

> When You said, "Seek My face [in prayer, require My presence as your greatest need]," my heart said to You, "Your face, O LORD, I will seek [on the authority of Your word]." (Psalm 27:8 AMP)

As life becomes busy and demanding, we can be aware of his beautiful presence everywhere we go. It becomes a moment by moment, non-stop awareness of God being in our midst doing life together with us. As we do this, we can eventually be like Smith Wigglesworth, who wouldn't go more than 15 minutes without talking with God, or like Enoch who was in constant touch with him.

> But as for me, my contentment is not in wealth but in seeing you and knowing all is well between us. (Psalm 17:15 TLB)

Prayer:

Dear Father, life can be so busy and demanding, yet I know, and I am thankful, that I do not have to walk in it alone. I have you by my side. Thank you for showing me how to walk with you on a continual basis just as Enoch did. Thank you for directing my steps. Thank you for helping me in my time of need and for hearing and answering my prayers. Dear Holy Spirit, please help me to be more aware of your beautiful presence in and through me.

CHAPTER 11

I will make an everlasting covenant with
them that I will do them good and not turn
away from them; and I will put in their heart a
fear and reverential awe of
Me, so that they will not turn away from Me

JEREMIAH 32:40 AMP

Between my junior and senior year of High School, I worked all summer long in order to buy a new stereo and my first Bible. The stereo goes without saying, since I don't remember a time when my love for music has not been there. The Bible, however, was a different story since I had no idea what to look for. I had never owned one, much less bought one. So, I opted on copying my friend's and I bought 'The Living Bible Paraphrased.' I was so proud of its green hardcover and my name engraved in gold letters. But truth be told, I found the thought of reading this mysterious book so puzzling. On the one hand I was excited, but on the other, I was a little nervous not knowing what I was going to find on the inside of those pages.

Coming from my catholic background, I figured it to be a book of do's and don'ts; something like the ten Commandments written in a hundred different ways. When I was younger, I remember being asked to draw a picture of my perception of God. After giving it some thought, my drawing culminated with a huge hand in the sky and its index finger pointing down from heaven in a condemning manner. As a whole, that was how I saw God.

I guess my curiosity had the best of me, so I was determined to find out what the Bible was all about by reading 10 pages a day, from cover to cover. As I began my quest for the truth, I must confess, the stories before my eyes sometimes left me flabbergasted. It was not about the rules I had previously anticipated, nor were they irrelevant stories for a teenage girl as myself. On the contrary, this great big God, who lived somewhere out in space, was portraying himself in a real and personal manner. Some of these stories were about actual people with real issues that I could even relate with.

Nonetheless, when I got to the Book of Proverbs, in my 16 year old mind, I translated the word for wisdom to mean being smart, which equated to good grades. I thought I had found the recipe for making effortless straight A's in school. I also noticed there were 31 chapters, so I began reading a corresponding chapter a day in addition to my ten original pages. Not surprisingly, this amazing book we know as the Bible became addictive to me. Throughout my days, I began looking forward to my time when I would get to read.

By the time I graduated from high school, I realized that learning about God's wisdom was greater than just good grades and human knowledge. Instead, I found God's wisdom to be powerful and able to deliver me out of my human limitations. This type of wisdom taught me how to live and act in every circumstance. It gave me warnings which have saved me from trouble and from the enemy's traps. It also helped me discern between good and evil (Proverbs 1:1-6).

And who wrote the Book of Proverbs, you may ask? It was no other than King Solomon, David's son, and the wisest and richest man who had ever lived on the earth (I Kings 3:5-13). So it goes without saying, that by reading and applying what it says, we are choosing to learn from the best.

REVERENCE THE LORD

Now, who in their right mind would not want to be wise? Almost from the beginning of the very first chapter in the Book of

Proverbs, King Solomon gave us the basic foundation for becoming wise. And it is so simple, we could actually miss it.

How does a man become wise? The first step is to trust and reverence the Lord! (Proverbs 1:7 TLB)

That is it...to trust and reverence the Lord! Some translations refer to it as: the fear of the Lord. Frankly, I believe much is said about trusting the Lord. However, I am concerned that very little is taught on the fear or reverence of God. Yet the Bible has much to say about it.

I know there can be some misconceptions on this topic. Just the other day my 15 year old son was telling me he was reading the Book of Proverbs, but did not understand what it meant to fear God. He asked, "Are we supposed to be afraid of God?" Thankfully, because I was already working on this chapter, I had enough information to give him an ear full.

FEAR

In most cases the word 'fear' has a negative connotation. And rightly so since this is how the devil's kingdom operates. Fear makes us want to run and hide from whatever, or whoever, we are afraid of. It is designed to paralyze us and make us ineffective. This type of fear is also meant to keep us from walking in God's divine plan for our lives.

The Bible mentions the word fear over 300 times. Normally a word or topic mentioned once in the Bible means it is important. But to see one brought up over 300 times means we should pay attention. In other words, knowing this is one of the devil's major tools of operation, we need to be ready at all times to stand against it. The Bible tells us not to be ignorant of his devices, therefore, we must be vigilant and watchful when fear tries to creep in (2 Corinthians 2:11).

Here are a few verses where the word fear is used and we are told not to fear:

Do not fear, for I am with you; do not be afraid, for I am your God. I will strengthen you; I will help you; I will hold on to you with my righteous right hand. (Isaiah 41:10 CSB)

Do not be afraid of sudden fear nor of the storm of the wicked when it comes...(Proverbs 3:25 AMP)

The LORD is my light and my salvation —whom should I fear? The LORD is the stronghold of my life —whom should I dread? (Psalms 27:1 CSB)

These are some of the ways the Bible translates the word fear from its original Hebrew and Greek roots: be afraid; terror; an awesome or terrifying thing (object causing fear); respect, reverence, piety; revered.

As a whole, fear is most often associated with terror, which can be a result of perceiving someone's power to do harm. This type of fear is often exploited through the things we watch, listen to, or participate in; things such as watching a horror movie, reading a scary book, playing with the occult or ouija boards, or even through listening to certain kinds of music, to name a few.

Engaging in evil is like sport to the fool [who refuses wisdom and chases sin], but to a man of understanding [skillful and godly] wisdom brings joy. What the wicked fears will come upon him, but the desire of the righteous [for the blessings of God] will be granted. (Proverbs 10:23-24 AMP)

Lets take for example something as recent as COVID-19. Everything about it was tailored to create fear (ie: the media, the masks, the lockdowns). People became crippled with abnormal and illogical fear. You could see fear in people's eyes as they stood behind a thick glass barrier with 3 layers of masks covering most of their faces. It was sheer terror for some, yet God was not in that fear. On the contrary, for those who sought his face, He was our very present help in times of trouble. He was our oasis in a dry and weary land.

He was the One we ran to and who kept us safe. The Bible lets us know that what most people fear is death. And the devil likes to use it to keep us from walking in the freedom and victory Jesus has already provided for us...

> *Jesus became human to fully identify with us. He did this, so that He could experience death and annihilate the effects of the intimidating accuser who holds against us the power of death. By embracing death Jesus sets free those who live their entire lives in bondage to the tormenting dread of death. (Hebrews 2:14-15 TPT)*

Knowing Jesus has already set us free from all that the enemy brings against us, we are to make a conscientious decision to resist fear at all times. One of my favorite Bible verses, and one I often quote when feeling fearful, is 2 Timothy 1:7:

> *For God has not given us a spirit of fear; but of power, and of love, and of a sound mind. (KJV)*

REVERENTIAL FEAR

If you seek skillful and godly wisdom as you would silver and search for her as you would hidden treasures;

> *Then you will understand the [reverent] fear of the LORD [that is, worshiping Him and regarding Him as truly awesome] and discover the knowledge of God. (Proverbs 2:4-5 AMP)*

For those who have chosen to please their heavenly Father, there is a reverential fear of God which brings delight to all the parties involved. For God's lovers, this is an attitude of respect and reverence toward their Creator. It is a foundational stance of pleasing our Lord and Father. In so doing, we purpose not to let anything get in the way of that; not sin, fear or disobedience. Instead, we seek to worship him with awe-inspired reverence and obedience.

How great is your goodness, which You have stored up for those who [reverently] fear You, which You have prepared for those who take refuge in You... (Psalm 31:19 AMP)

Reverence for the Lord is a fountain of life; its waters keep a man from death. (Proverbs 14:27 TLB)

But the eyes of the Lord are watching over those who fear Him, who rely upon his steady love. He will keep them from death even in times of famine! (Psalm 33:18-19 TLB)

REVERED

As a nation who fought and won its independence from England's monarchy long ago, I venture to say most of us are not familiar with the fear, the respect, and the awe that comes from that type of rulership. For instance, throughout the Bible there are many examples of kings, both weak and strong, who were feared simply because they had the power to take people's lives on a whim. To our detriment, with our culture being so far removed from this manner of life, I believe we have transferred our lack of reverence, respect and awe for earthly authority into our relationship with God.

Although our fear of God is not to be confused with the fear of men, or the fear of God's judgment for those who choose evil, there is the side of it we must be willing to pursue. The following Proverb gives us a good taste of what this looks like:

The [reverent] fear of the LORD [that is, worshiping Him and regarding Him as truly awesome] is the beginning and the preeminent part of wisdom [its starting point and its essence], and the knowledge of the Holy One is understanding and spiritual insight. (Proverbs 9:10 AMP)

This reverential fear comes from knowing that God alone is King and LORD of our lives. Jesus, as our ultimate example, did not follow his own plans or wishes, but instead, He looked to the Father for his every move (John 5:19). Pleasing and obeying his Father was the motivation behind everything He did. Jesus revered his Father so much, He surrendered to a brutal death on a cross just to please him. The Father was his all and all!

Worship in awe and wonder, all you who've been made holy!
For all who fear him will feast with plenty. (Psalm 34:9 TPT)

Like Jesus, we are to let our reverence of God lead and motivate everything we do. As a generation of God Pleasers, our job is to worship our Creator in awe and wonder! To regard him as truly awesome.

HATRED OF EVIL

The [reverent] fear and worshipful awe of the LORD includes
the hatred of evil; Pride and arrogance and the evil way, and
the perverted mouth, I hate. (Proverbs 8:13 AMP)

Since we do not see God with our physical eyes, some might forget that He is ever present and all knowing. I venture to say that at times, even Christians act and do things as if God is not around. However, in order to walk in a manner pleasing to God, I believe we are to love what God loves and hate what God hates. Evil is one of those things we must never tolerate in our lives. It is often in the small, or seemingly insignificant things we do, which reflect the state of our hearts in this matter. It is also evident in the way we act behind closed doors, when we think no one is watching. Or in the manner in which we conduct our business or treat others when we think we are the only authority present.

Wisdom pours into you when you begin to hate every form of evil in your life, for that's what worship and fearing God is all about. (Proverbs 8:13 TPT)

By choosing to become Modern Day Enoch's, a people who reflect the reverential fear of God, it is going to take more than just desiring it and crying out for it. It will require that we walk in a total surrendered life with zero tolerance for evil, pride, and any form of perversion.

A TERRIFYING THING

*For we know the one who has said, Vengeance belongs to me; I will repay, and again, The Lord will judge his people.
It is a terrifying thing to fall into the hands of the living God. (Hebrews 10:30-31 CSB)*

There is also the side of fear that is frightful and terrifying. This type of fear belongs to those who follow after evil and wickedness; those who oppress the weak and vulnerable. There is a time when God says "enough," and at that time, woe to those who have followed after evil for they will experience God's judgment.

Who knows the power of your anger? For as the fear of You, so is your wrath. (Psalm 90:11 NKJV)

But how different are the wicked. All they are is dust in the wind—driven away to destruction! The wicked will not endure the day of judgment, for God will not defend them. Nothing they do will succeed or endure for long, for they have no part with those who walk in truth. (Psalm 1:4-5 TPT)

The flood is an example of this terrifying fear in which every living thing, except for those inside the ark, were completely wiped out.

At the Flood, the Lord showed his control of all creation. Now
He continues to unveil his power. (Psalm 29:10 TLB)

There are many other instances in the Bible where God's judgment
came to deal with evil. For instance, when the earth opened its
mouth and swallowed people alive, or when burning sulfur rained
from the sky destroying complete cities (Numbers 16:32 and Genesis
19:24). Such is the fate for those who choose to walk in the ways of
the ungodly. Unless they repent and turn from their wicked ways,
God's judgment will come and it will be pure terror for them.

BROADCAST HIS WONDERS

Something unique about Enoch that we find in the Book of Jude
is the following:

Enoch, the seventh direct descendant from Adam, prophesied of
their doom when he said, "Look! Here comes the Lord Yahweh
with his countless myriads of holy ones.
He comes to execute judgment against them all and to convict
each one of them for their ungodly deeds and for all the
terrible words that ungodly sinners have spoken against him."
(Jude 14-15 TPT)

Remember, Enoch lived and walked with God in a consistent
and dedicated manner for 300 years. He was a man who understood
and believed God is good and a rewarder of those who do good.
Through this scripture, however, we get to see a side of Enoch that
has to do with his level of obedience to God. Not only did he not
tolerate sin, but he was vocal in his conviction. When it came to
sinners, he did not remain silent. We are told that he prophesied and
preached a hard message of God's coming judgment and the need to
repent for those walking in sin.

If we are to please God with our lives, we not only have to hate
all that is evil, but we are to show others the way to Jesus through

repentance and freedom from sin. No longer can we sit on the sidelines and allow deception to reign in our culture by allowing evil to be called good and good evil. We must call sin for what it is. We cannot be concerned with offending people who are on their way to hell. Instead, when the Holy Spirit nudges us to talk to someone, or prophecy to them, let us be quick to obey and speak the truth in love and with boldness.

...that you may declare the praise of Him who called you out of darkness into his wonderful light. (1 Peter 2:9 NIV)

The Bible calls us Christ's ambassadors (2 Corinthians 5:20 NIV). That means we are his representatives here on earth. In other words, when people see us, they should be able to see the One we represent. As his ambassadors, we have been chosen to, "...broadcast his glorious wonders throughout the world" (1 Peter 2:9 TPT). We are his special possession and carriers of his treasures! We take his promises and share the wonderful news with others. We are created to display his beauty and love everywhere we go. In this, we bring great pleasure to our Master and King.

But I enter your house by the abundance of your faithful love; I bow down toward your holy temple in reverential awe of You. (Psalm 5:7 CSB)

FEAR OF MAN

The fear of mankind is a snare, but the one who trusts in the LORD is protected. (Proverbs 29:25 CSB)

From the time we are little we are trained to be people pleasers. Many of us grow up being taught to please our parents and gain their approval. From there, we move on to wanting to please our teachers, and eventually our friends and those we deem important. The problem comes when the desire to please people keeps us from obeying God. This is the fear of man. As the scripture says, the fear of man is a snare. Therefore, we cannot have this kind of fear alongside the fear of God. We will either fear God or fear men.

I am reminded of my years growing up in Mexico when the pope would visit the nation. People idolized the man. They plastered his picture everywhere, lit candles to him, and treated him with unquestionable reverence. It was not uncommon for businesses and schools to close their doors in order to follow his every move. Those who did not live in the areas he visited became glued to their television sets just to catch a glimpse. Organizations and venues prepared months in advance with parades, children's choirs, and other special events. No expense was spared as I watched the nation go all out for a man.

At present, we don't need to look too far to see this type of outlandish behavior. Just walk into a concert or a sports event. Stadiums have to be some of the wildest and loudest places to exist. People are willing to spend hundreds of dollars to participate in sporting events. Even more, I think we have all heard of those who faint at the presence of the person they idolize. The problem is that we were not made to revere men or other spiritual entities. This need to be in awe and in admiration of someone is only meant to be directed towards our only King, Jesus.

If we as humans are already prepared to extravagantly admire people, why is it so outlandish to raise our hands, worship and dance before the King of Kings? There is no need to judge your resident church yeller or worship dancer. Is not the One who formed us and nurtured us, worthy of our full reverence and awe?

> *Therefore, since we are receiving a kingdom that cannot be shaken, let us be thankful. By it, we may serve God acceptably, with reverence and awe, for our God is a consuming fire. (Hebrews 12:28-29 CSB)*

WHAT WE VALUE

There is much to be said and learned about the reverential fear of God. However, as we begin to understand and walk in it, I am convinced it will draw us closer to our King, helping us to experience his loving kindness in ways that we have not yet known. Just think, whatever level of respect we give someone or something is a reflection of the value we have for them or for it. If I do not value a certain object, no matter its cost or importance, I will treat it poorly and maybe even ruin it, causing it to lose its original value. In the same manner, the reverential fear of God is like a thermometer that measures how much or how little we value God's presence. Something else to take note of, the same manner in which we choose to value God, He will reveal himself to us!

But his joy is in those who reverence him, those who expect him to be loving and kind. (Psalm 147:11 TLB)

SOLOMON'S CONCLUSION

The Book of Proverbs begins and ends with the reverential fear of God. In the second to last verse we find Solomon concluding his theory of the virtuous woman with the following:

Charm can be deceptive and beauty doesn't last, but a woman who fears and reverences God shall be greatly praised. (Proverbs 31:30 TLB)

It is to be noted that this whole section on the Proverbs 31 woman can be a representation of the Bride of Christ, meaning us. There is so much to learn from these verses, but let it suffice to say that our religious works or good deeds can be deceptive. Yet our reverential fear of God is eternal.

Interestingly enough, also in the second to last verse of the Book of Ecclesiastes, which is also written by Solomon, he concludes his whole inquiring journey on the meaning of life with the following:

> Here is my final conclusion: fear God and obey his commandments, for this is the entire duty of man. (Ecclesiastes 12:13 TLB)

After touching on so many areas on obtaining wisdom and pursuing happiness, Solomon's conclusion is the same in both of the books he wrote, fear God. In Ecclesiastes, he explores topics such as: wealth, pleasure, religion, politics and human wisdom. Each time he reassures the reader that they are all futile. After all is said and done, his verdict is the same...the only thing that matters in life is our reverential worship and obedience to God.

In my opinion, through both books, Solomon is trying to save us from wasting years, or even a lifetime, with things we presume will bring us happiness. In the end, the only thing which will satisfy our heart's deep longing is our reverential fear of God. I know it sounds so simple, but when we become reverent and in awe of him, it changes the way we look at life and how we carry ourselves. Our dreams, pursuits, and desires begin to take on his perfect plans for our lives. And this is indeed where we begin a life of true contentment, a life well lived and a life that is truly satisfying and pleasing to him!

> O taste and see that the LORD [our God] is good; How blessed [fortunate, prosperous, and favored by God] is the man who takes refuge in Him...For to those who fear Him there is no want. (Psalm 34:8-9b AMP)

In Psalm 12 David declares this truth so beautifully:

> O God-Enthroned in heaven, I lift my eyes toward you in worship. The way I love you is like the way a servant wants to please his master, the way a maid waits for the orders of her mistress. We look to you, our God, with passionate longing

to please you and discover more of your mercy and grace.
(Psalm 123:1-2 TPT)

Prayer;

Dear Heavenly Father, I want to be pleasing to you with every part of my being. I desire to grow in the fear and awe of you and I long to have you be the focus of all my attention. Teach me to give you the reverence and respect that is due you. And as I grow in the knowledge and fear of you, may it become contagious to all those around me.

CHAPTER 12

He brought me out into a broad place; He rescued me because **He was pleased with me and delighted in me**

PSALM 18:19 AMP

hroughout the pages of the Bible we are made privy to different people's relationship with God. At times I feel as if I am watching a television series on a multi-generational line of people whose common thread is God. All have the equal gift of freewill and get to choose their own quest in life. Many choose to go after vain pursuits, while a few follow the narrow path we seldom hear read:

> *"Come to God through the narrow gate, because the wide gate and broad path is the way that leads to destruction—nearly everyone chooses that crowded road! The narrow gate and the difficult way leads to eternal life—so few even find it!" (Matthew 7:13-14 TPT)*

People sometimes complain and walk away from Christianity because they say it is too hard. My experience, however, is that when we step out of a religious mindset and trying to please men rather than God, Christianity is the easiest and most satisfying path there is. I find it so reassuring to know that when we walk with Jesus, we are never alone. We don't have to encounter anything on our own.

And whereas people are fickle, God has promised to never leave us nor forsake us.

> *...He has said, "I WILL NEVER [under any circumstances] DESERT YOU [nor give you up nor leave you without support, nor will I in any degree leave you helpless], NOR WILL I FORSAKE or LET YOU DOWN or RELAX MY HOLD ON YOU [assuredly not]!" (Hebrews 13:5 AMP)*

What a most wonderful promise! This was the very first Scripture I remember memorizing. It spoke volumes to me knowing that there was someone who would always be there for me...and these many years later, this same verse still has that same effect.

"I DID MY BEST FOR YOU, DADDY!"

After graduating from high school, I took a winter job as a ski instructor. Although teaching others to ski is not as fun as actual skiing, it was so rewarding to help others experience the joy and passion I felt coming down a mountain on skis.

As with any sport or hobby, everyone comes into it with a different motive. Some learn this sport because they are told to do it since it is a "family" tradition, yet there are others who can hardly wait to learn the ropes of a new adventure. It did not take me long to realize that people's ability to learn is greatly determined by their motive. Those whose hearts were not in it, or were scared, had the hardest time getting on their skies. Some even gave up before they could experience the wonders, beauty and thrill of skiing.

Many years later, the memory of a particular little girl remains engraved in my mind. This wee girl started from scratch, without any previous experience. She learned how to walk in those awkward ski boots, to put her skis on, ride the ski lift and, eventually, was able to come down the slope making turns and stopping on demand. Helping her accomplish that was so satisfying! But even more so was the memory of what took place next. After she had been picked up by her parents, I was able to watch her ski down to her dad from my chair lift. As she did, she hollered: "I did my best for you, Daddy! I did my best for you!"

Now that was truly satisfying! Seeing the delight in her little face as she skied to her dad left me with a most beautiful image of what our relationship with our heavenly Father can look like. I could not see her father's face, but I can only imagine what must have been going on inside of him. As a father, he must have been so pleased to see his little princess delight in what he delighted in. He must have felt so proud of her and, at the same time, must have basked in her admiration and desire to please him. How much more so our heavenly father as we live to please him.

FOR YOUR PLEASURE WE WERE CREATED

Thou art worthy, O Lord, to receive glory and honor and power: for thou hast created all things, and for thy pleasure they are and were created. (Revelation 4:11 KJV)

Not long ago I heard a minister share a personal story on the radio. He was sharing about an afternoon he had come home tired from a long day's work. After dinner, he grabbed a glass of ice tea and went out to his backyard to relax and watch as his children played. A little later, when his wife came to tell the kids to go inside and start getting ready for bed, their oldest daughter approached her mom and asked if they could play a little longer. When her mom asked for a reason, their daughter explained, "Because dad is delighting in us."

She had perceived it well. He had been delighting in them as they played and had fun with each other. They were just being kids and doing what kids do. Yet that was enough to bring delight to their father. Isn't it so wonderful that as God's children, we too, can bring him so much pleasure and delight?

When people turn to you, they discover how easy you are to please—so faithful and true! Joyfully you teach them the proper path, even when they go astray. (Psalm 25:8 TPT)

YOU ARE MY CHOICE

My choice is you, God, first and only. And now I find I'm your choice! (Psalm 16:5 MESS)

If anyone ever believed pleasing God was impossible, Enoch proved them wrong. Before he was taken, never to be seen again, he received the testimony of having walked with God and of pleasing him. He did it! He believed God was good and a rewarder of those who diligently seek him (Hebrews 11:6). In short, Enoch walked with God, had constant communion with him, and pleased him. Let us follow suit!

Although God did not give us much details on how Enoch specifically pleased him, we can discover many clues throughout the Bible of how to do this. But we must search for what that looks like in each of our own lives. So it is up to us to find our own path, born out of relationship with him! It is up to us to accept his constant invitations and reminders of his tender love for us. It is up to us to seek his face until our hearts melt with passion for more of him.

Much like Enoch, Moses and David did, we must take our turn approaching our King and seeking his face day and night. And just as deep calls unto deep in each of their hearts, let us go deep into our quest and desire to please him (Psalm 42:7).

HE FULLY HAS ME

He is within me—I am his garden of delight. I have Him fully and now He fully has me! (Song of Songs 6:3 TPT)

As time continues, our cravings for him increase. It is then we become His garden of delight. We are like that rose that He comes to see every morning and evening for pure pleasure. Whatever we purpose in our hearts to offer him is worth its full investment! It is worth every bit of the sacrifices and the cost!

> *I long to drink of you, O God, to drink deeply from the streams of pleasure flowing from your presence. My longings overwhelm me for more of you! My soul thirsts, pants, and longs for the living God. I want to come and see the face of God. (Psalm 42:1-2 TPT)*

This is where I believe Enoch lived! He was constantly in God's presence! He lived, walked, and breathed God. His life became a pleasure to God. I believe God is awakening in his people a passion much like Enoch's. But instead of one man, He is calling an army. He is calling his army of believers to walk with him in a way that we have never known or experienced before, in such closeness and intimacy. And it all starts with a desire and a hunger for more of him, and a holy dissatisfaction for anything else. A craving for more of his presence! A longing to walk and talk with him face to face.

This new army is not one that is out to serve their own passions, but those of their Commander in Chief! They are dissatisfied with the fake, and with anything resembling man's ways. They want what is true and real and will settle for nothing less. Their faces are set like flint to do the will of their Master! (Isaiah 50:7)

This new, rising army will be known as the generation who pleased their God!!!...And you, my friend, have been enlisted!

> *...We've kept you always in our prayers that you would receive the perfect knowledge of God's pleasure over your lives, making you reservoirs of every kind of wisdom and spiritual understanding. We pray that you would walk in the ways of true righteousness, pleasing God in every good thing you do. Then you'll become fruit bearing branches, yielding to his life and maturing in the rich experience of knowing God in his fullness! (Colossians 1:9-10 TPT)*

Prayer:

Dear God, help me to walk as a fruit bearing branch, yielded to you and growing in knowledge and experience of your fullness. May I walk daily in revelation of your pleasure over my life; and may I walk in the ways of true righteousness, pleasing you in every good thing I do, Amen!

Printed in the United States
by Baker & Taylor Publisher Services